WEEKDAY
Gourmet

WEEKDAY
Gourmet

HEALTHFUL, DELICIOUS MEALS
IN 30 MINUTES OR LESS

LINDA FERRARI

Prima Publishing

PRIMA PUBLISHING and colophon are registered trademarks of Prima Communications, Inc.

Illustrations © 1996 by Diane Clark

Library of Congress Cataloging-in-Publication Data

Ferrari, Linda.
Weekday gourmet: healthful, delicious meals in 30 minutes or less / by Linda Ferrari.
p. cm.
Includes index.
ISBN 0-7615-0404-4
1. Quick and easy cookery. 2. Dinners and dining. I. Title.
TX833.5.F47 1996

641.5'55—dc20   96-13168
                                                                CIP

96 97 98 99 00 AA 10 9 8 7 6 5 4 3 2
Printed in the United States of America

ABOUT THE NUTRITIONAL ANALYSES

A per serving nutritional breakdown is provided for each recipe. If a range is given for an ingredient amount, the breakdown is based on the smaller number. If a range is given for servings, the breakdown is based on the larger number. If a choice of ingredients is given in an ingredient listing, the breakdown is calculated using the first choice. Nutritional content may vary depending on the specific brands or types of ingredients used. For anaylizing these recipes, all mayonnaise used was lowfat; all milk, cream cheese, and sour cream was nonfat; all soy sauce was low sodium; and all broth used was defatted. "Optional" ingredients or those for which no specific amount is stated are not included in the breakdown.

HOW TO ORDER:

Single copies may be ordered from Prima Publishing, P.O. Box 1260BK, Rocklin, CA 95677; telephone (916) 632-4400. Quantity discounts are also available. On your letterhead, include information concerning the intended use of the books and the number of books you wish to purchase.

Visit us online at http://www.primapublishing.com

To my family, who always supports
and makes possible all that I dream of doing.

Thank you to

my husband,
Phil,

my sons,
Philip and T. J.,

and my daughters,
Cindy, Michelle, Suzy, and Carrie.

I love you all.

Contents

Acknowledgments   xiii
Introduction   xv

Chapter One
APPETIZERS

Chapter Two
SOUPS

Chapter Three
SALADS

Chapter Four
MAIN DISHES

Chapter Five
SIDE DISHES

Chapter Six
DESSERTS

Acknowledgments

The process of writing a cookbook and all the steps to finally seeing it on bookstore shelves are very complicated. I write the text and recipes and then many other people enter the scene to complete the book. I want to thank everyone at Prima Publishing for letting me do this book and for all the help I got along the way. Jennifer Basye Sander deserves special thanks for all her help, understanding, and encouragement. Thanks to my project editor, Debra Venzke; Rosaleen Bertolino for copyediting; Tackett-Barbaria Design for the beautiful cover; and to my friend Diane Clark for the interior artwork and the beautiful artwork in my kitchen. And lastly I want to give a very special thanks to my agent, Linda Hayes, who is always there for me.

Introduction

I cater, write books, teach cooking, do cooking spots on television, and, most importantly, have a large family that I take great joy in cooking for. I also love spending hours in the kitchen experimenting and creating new dishes. By now you may think that I am a little crazy. Well, that is probably true, as I have obviously chosen cooking for my life's work. But after days on end of cooking, even I like a quick, delicious meal that gets me out of my kitchen fast, yet satisfies my family. This book will help you to accomplish this same feat.

We are so busy with jobs, family, and activities that a repertoire of quick and healthful recipes is essential. One survey found that most families have a collection of no more than twenty recipes, which they cook over and over again for family and friends. Think about it, I bet that this is fairly accurate for most of us.

The recipes in this book are not only quick, but are nutritionally sound, paying attention to sodium, cholesterol, and fat content. As you shop, stock up on products such as low-sodium broth, low-sodium soy sauce, low-sodium salt, egg substitute, nonfat dairy items, and heart-smart oils and spreads.

BASICS OF QUICK, HEALTHFUL COOKING

USE BROTH INSTEAD OF BUTTER

Instead of sautéing onions, garlic, or vegetables in butter, slowly cook them in broth until the liquid evaporates. This method develops a rich and satisfying flavor.

Vegetable Oil Sprays

Put fresh virgin olive oil, sesame oil, chili oil, walnut oil, and other oils into small spray bottles for greasing skillets and oiling baking pans. The spray bottles produce a very fine mist of oil and therefore you use less, resulting in fewer calories and less fat. Vegetable oil sprays also are available in grocery stores and you may choose to use those instead.

Use Small Amounts of the Real Thing

I love the taste and smell of real butter; sometimes the smallest amount can contribute a lovely flavor, smoothness, or sheen to a sauce that you cannot get in any other way. By shaving, grating, or shredding Parmesan and other flavorful cheeses, you can extend their flavor while keeping the dish relatively low in fat.

If you must have butter on your potatoes or salt on your meat, then I suggest adding it at the last moment. When you can see the small pat of butter (¼ to ½ teaspoon) on your potato or the glistening of the salt crystals on your meat, your mind and taste buds will be happy, while you will have cut down on the amount of fat and sodium you are using. Eventually, you will be so pleased with all the new flavor you find in your food (because you are not masking taste with fat), you won't need the visual satisfaction that fat and salt give you.

Kosher salt or sea salt are called for in many of the recipes. These salts are large, flaky crystals that look attractive, have less additives, and sea salt still has natural minerals left in it. In addition, because they are more intense in flavor than standard table salt, they can, and should be, used sparingly.

Use a Variety of Ingredients

Once you take away the rich taste and texture that fat lends to foods, you have to find ways to replace it. If you don't add enough ingredients, you will not have a satisfying result. Think about a recipe calling for meat, water, onion, salt, and pepper.

Where will the flavor and interest come from if you do not add herbs, spices, wines, or an array of delicious vegetables? A quick meal need not be a dull one. Stock your kitchen with the staples listed below, try the recipes in this book, and learn to experiment.

HOW TO USE THIS BOOK

Start out by just thumbing through this book from cover to cover, marking recipes that interest you and your family. Then read over the following pantry supply pages and pick out the items you want to start with. If your family does not like curry, dried tomatoes, or black-eyed peas, then of course you do not need to stock these items.

FILLING YOUR PANTRY, REFRIGERATOR, AND FREEZER

Keeping your pantry, freezer, and refrigerator well-stocked is the only way to create quick, delicious, and healthful meals. It is imperative that you have a pantry full of supplies so that when you are in a hurry, everything will be at your fingertips. Keeping your pantry and freezer well-stocked is pretty easy, but it takes time to fill the refrigerator each week with fresh, high-quality ingredients. Wonderful fresh herbs, assorted wild and domestic mushrooms, fresh jalapeños, colorful peppers, and a variety of fruits and vegetables need frequent replacing, and they are essential in creating texture and interest in these recipes. With proper handling and wrapping, these items can stay fresh throughout the week. Other staples such as butter, nonfat sour cream, nonfat cream cheese, and other dairy products will need replacing less frequently.

It is important to add bursts of unusual flavors to familiar ones in order to heighten our eating experience. That is why such items as herbs, spices, oils, vinegars, fire-roasted peppers, seedless raspberry jam, and liquid smoke are so important to the outcome of a dish. Most dried spices and herbs will last six months if tightly sealed and kept in a dry, dark place. If you don't foresee using an herb that quickly, you could always ask a friend or two to split a bottle of spice with you.

Also remember, if you don't have the herb called for on hand, it's OK to substitute another. For instance, if a recipe calls for oregano and you don't have it, try using basil or rosemary instead. You may even decide that you prefer the spice you used. This rule of substitution holds true for vegetable ingredients as well; just use the vegetables you have on hand and don't worry. Have fun when you cook and don't stress over minor details. Improvisation is what makes great cooks who delight in the process of cooking.

PANTRY GOODS

(some items will need refrigeration after opening)

flour	cake flour
baking powder	baking soda
white sugar	brown sugar
cornstarch	oatmeal
nonfat granola	dried mushrooms
potatoes	onions and garlic
dried tomato seasoning	seedless raspberry jam
clam juice	canned corn kernels
dried tomatoes	hoisin sauce
low-sodium soy sauce	Worcestershire sauce
prepared mustards	horseradish
dried pastas	long grain rice
arborio rice	honey
garlic paste	broth (chicken, beef, vegetable)
kosher and sea salt	fish sauce
corn flake crumbs	lowfat refried beans
quick-cooking couscous	canned beans (white, black, kidney)
canned diced chilies	fire-roasted bell peppers
chipotle chilies in adobo sauce	evaporated skim milk
dried ancho chilies	premade polenta
olives	

Tabasco

tomato paste

curry paste

cornstarch

peach and apricot nectar

capers

Kitchen Bouquet seasoning

flavored oils (*walnut, sesame, virgin olive, garlic, chili, hazelnut, avocado, peanut*)

flavored vinegars (*cider, champagne, fruit-flavored, red wine, rice, herb, balsamic*)

canned beets

black-eyed peas

nonfat Italian dressing

catsup

lowfat coconut milk

lowfat mayonnaise

HERBS AND SPICES

lemon pepper	red pepper flakes	peppercorns
tarragon	bay leaves	coriander
ground ginger	onion powder	garlic powder
paprika	ground cloves	cream of tartar
dill	thyme leaves	basil leaves
saffron or turmeric	marjoram	fennel seed
Old Bay seasoning	dried chives	cayenne
cumin	sesame seeds	chili powder
aniseed	allspice	cinnamon
nutmeg	sage	celery seed
rosemary	chervil	

EXTRACTS

vanilla	almond	rum
lemon	orange	maple

DRIED FRUITS AND NUTS

dried cranberries	dried blueberries	dried cherries
raisins	slivered almonds	pine nuts
walnuts	black walnuts	pecans

WINE, LIQUORS, AND LIQUEURS

port	dry sherry	white wine
Calvados (or applejack)	cassis	marsala wine
rum	amaretto	whiskey
brandy	chardonnay	cabernet

FROZEN ITEMS

flash-frozen chicken breasts
flash-frozen shrimp
flash-frozen white fish
flash-frozen lobster pieces

hash browns	phyllo pastry	asparagus
spinach	frozen juice concentrates	whipped topping

REFRIGERATOR ITEMS

nonfat yogurts (vanilla, lemon, toffee, and plain)
dry cheeses (Asiago, Parmesan, Romano, pecorino, dry jack,
   Kasseri, or Mitzithra)

fruits and vegetables	nonfat milk	nonfat buttermilk
nonfat sour cream	nonfat cream cheese	nonfat cottage cheese
eggs	egg substitute	butter
fresh herbs	lettuces	feta cheese

soup base (both chicken and beef)*

---

*A tablespoon of this thrown into soups, stews, gravies, or sauces really makes a difference. I use the chicken soup base that I buy from discount food and household stores. It will keep in the refrigerator for a couple of months. You can make as little or as much as you like based on the following recipe:

1 cup granular chicken soup base	2 tablespoons dried marjoram
1 tablespoon dried onion flakes	2 tablespoons dried thyme
1 tablespoon dried green pepper flakes	2 tablespoons dried parsley
1 tablespoon dried tomato seasoning	Lots of coarsely ground black pepper

Chapter One

APPETIZERS

When you need a quick appetizer for unexpected guests, try some of the following fast and delicious recipes. The chapter starts with some tasty dips and spreads and then moves on to heartier appetizers, such as potstickers and biscuits. When you're having a big dinner party, give yourself a head start and pick up some precooked or precut items from your local market. You can find the vegetables used in some of these appetizers already sliced at your grocery's salad bar; pick up some steamed rice at a Chinese take-out for the Rice and Canadian Bacon Squares. When time is of the essence, it is amazing how organized you become.

GARDEN PLATTER WITH TARRAGON-MUSTARD DIP

Makes about 1 1/4 cups.

The suggested vegetables for this platter can all be enjoyed raw to save you the trouble and time of blanching, but feel free to substitute any vegetables you like.

Choose three or four of the following vegetables:
Fresh fennel bulbs, cut in
  wedges
Baby carrots
Raw baby beets, julienned
Broccoli, cut into flowerets
English cucumbers, cut into
  thin diagonal slices
Peppers, cut into thin strips
Radishes, cleaned and ends
  removed
Squash, cut into thin sticks
Cherry tomatoes
Turnips, peeled and cut into
  thin sticks
Jicama, peeled and cut into
  thin sticks

Celery, cut into thin sticks
Cauliflower, cut into flowerets
Snow peas
Young green beans

Dip ingredients:
  2 tablespoons chopped
     fresh tarragon, or 2
     teaspoons dried
  1 cup nonfat sour cream
  1 tablespoon lowfat
     mayonnaise
1 to 2 teaspoons cider vinegar
  1 tablespoon Dijon
     mustard, or to taste
  1 teaspoon lemon pepper
     Salt to taste

Prepare the vegetables and display on a pretty plate or in a basket.

Mix all dip ingredients together and spoon into a pretty bowl or hollowed-out bell pepper and serve with the vegetables. You can prepare the dip a day ahead. In that case, cover and refrigerate it until ready to use.

Each serving (one tablespoon of dip) provides
10 calories   0.9 g protein   1 g carbohydrate   0.4 g fat
0 g dietary fiber   75 mg sodium   1 mg cholesterol

CHILI-CUCUMBER DUNK

Makes about 1¹/₂ cups.

A refreshing dip that's great for a summer party.

1 bottled fire-roasted red pepper, puréed in a food processor	1 small fresh Anaheim chili, minced
¼ cup nonfat sour cream	1 small tomato, seeded and diced small
1 tablespoon lowfat mayonnaise	2 tablespoons chopped cilantro
1 English cucumber, peeled, halved, and seeds scraped out	2 cloves garlic, minced Salt and lemon pepper to taste

Blend the pepper, sour cream, and mayonnaise. Dice the cucumber very small and blend the cucumber and all the remaining ingredients into the sour cream mixture. Spoon into a crock or hollowed-out bell pepper. Serve with toast points, crackers, or raw vegetables.

Each serving (one tablespoon) provides
8 calories   0.4 g protein   1.3 g carbohydrate   0.2 g fat
0.3 g dietary fiber   19 mg sodium   0 mg cholesterol

FETA-CHARD SPREAD

Makes 1¹/2 cups.

You can make this delicious spread a day ahead if necessary. Serve it with vegetables, toast points, crackers, or cooked shrimp.

2 leeks, white part only, sliced
1½ tablespoons olive oil
1 cup chopped raw chard
1 bottled fire-roasted red pepper

1 cup nonfat sour cream
2 tablespoons feta cheese
Salt and pepper to taste

Sauté the leeks in the olive oil until leeks are soft. Add the chard and cook, stirring, for 1 minute. Put leeks and chard into a food processor. Add the pepper and run processor for 10 seconds. Add the sour cream, feta, and salt and pepper to taste, then pulse processor a few times to just blend. Refrigerate until ready to use.

Each serving (one tablespoon) provides
16 calories   0.8 g protein   1.2 g carbohydrate   0.9 g fat
0.1 g dietary fiber   28 mg sodium   1 mg cholesterol

OLIVE AND PEPPER SPREAD

Makes about 2 cups spread.

This is an attractive spread with a very distinctive flavor. Serve with crostini or pita triangles.

1 cup niçoise olives
1 cup kalamata olives
½ cup green Greek-style olives
½ yellow bell pepper
½ red bell pepper

¼ cup chopped fresh basil
3 tablespoons minced red onion
2 teaspoons virgin olive oil
Sea salt and pepper to taste

Pit and mince the olives. Mince the peppers and mix them with the olives in a bowl. Add the basil, onion, and oil. Season with salt and pepper to taste.

Each serving (one tablespoon) provides
47 calories   0.1 g protein   1.2 g carbohydrate   4.8 g fat
0.4 g dietary fiber   280 mg sodium   0 mg cholesterol

MUSHROOM AND ANCHO CHILI PÂTÉ

Makes about 1 cup pâté.

This pâté is fantastic spread on toast, crackers, or crostini. Reconstituted dried ancho chilies are also wonderful in sauces and dips.

1 small dried ancho chili
1 portobello mushroom, chopped
6 ounces chanterelle, shiitake, or white mushrooms, chopped
½ onion, chopped
2 cloves garlic, minced
2 tablespoons brandy

2 teaspoons butter
1 teaspoon dried thyme
1 teaspoon dried chervil
2 tablespoons evaporated skim milk
3 tablespoons nonfat cream cheese
Salt and pepper to taste

Reconstitute the chili by covering with warm water until chili softens, about 10 minutes.

In a nonstick pan, sauté the mushrooms, onion, and garlic in the brandy and butter until the liquid from the mushrooms evaporates. Drain the chili and put the chili and the mushroom mixture into a processor or blender and purée. Stir in the thyme, chervil, milk, and cream cheese. Add salt and pepper to taste. Pack the mixture into a small bowl and press down firmly. Cover and refrigerate or serve immediately. (Can be made the day before.)

Each serving provides
20 calories   1.1 g protein   2.3 g carbohydrate   0.6 g fat
0.4 g dietary fiber   24 mg sodium   2 mg cholesterol

ROASTED PEPPER PÂTÉ WITH FETA

Makes about 2¹/₄ cups.

All the ingredients for this fast and easy pâté can be on hand and ready to go for last-minute guests.

1 (6-ounce) jar fire-roasted red peppers, drained
1 (4-ounce) can chopped, roasted jalapeños, drained
½ onion, cut in half again

1 (4-ounce) can chopped black olives
¾ cup nonfat sour cream
2 ounces feta cheese
Sea salt and pepper to taste

Put all ingredients into a food processor and whirl until all ingredients are puréed. Press ingredients into a crock and cover with plastic wrap. Press down heavily and evenly on pâté and refrigerate for at least 20 minutes. Serve with crackers or toast points.

Each serving (one tablespoon) provides
13 calories   0.7 g protein   1.1 g carbohydrate   0.8 g fat
0.2 g dietary fiber   109 mg sodium   2 mg cholesterol

Marinated Peppers and Shrimp

Makes about 8 servings.

A supply of cooked frozen shrimp in the freezer helps you make meals quickly. Serve this dish in a pretty bowl to make a colorful presentation.

1 pound frozen, cooked shrimp, thawed and rinsed

½ cup slivered, marinated bell peppers

12 snow peas, strings removed, blanched in boiling water for 1 minute

2 tablespoons minced red onion

¼ cup rice vinegar

1 tablespoon virgin olive oil

2 teaspoons sugar

1 tablespoon chopped fresh dill, or 1 teaspoon dried Sea salt and pepper to taste

Toss together the shrimp, peppers, snow peas, and red onion. Whisk together the vinegar, oil, sugar, and dill and season with salt and pepper to taste. Sprinkle over the shrimp mixture and blend well. Let sit at least 10 minutes before serving.

Each serving provides
111 calories   12.2 g protein   2.5 g carbohydrate   5.7 g fat
0.4 g dietary fiber   170 mg sodium   111 mg cholesterol

CRAB ON CRISPY NOODLE ROUNDS

Makes about 20 appetizers.

All kinds of things are wonderful on these irresistible noodle rounds. Instead of the crab mixture given here, try finely diced chicken with goat cheese and dried tomatoes, or a mixture of slivered vegetables moistened with soy sauce and sesame oil and a touch of five-spice powder.

⅓ pound dried vermicelli, broken into 3-inch pieces
3 green onions, finely diced
¼ cup finely diced red bell pepper
1 egg
  Celery salt and freshly ground pepper to taste
½ pound cooked white crabmeat, drained if canned

2 small fresh jalapeños, minced
½ cup chopped cilantro
1 small tomato, seeded and finely diced
3 tablespoons rice vinegar
2 tablespoons lowfat mayonnaise
  Vegetable oil spray

Cook vermicelli until al dente and drain. In a bowl, mix together the vermicelli, green onions, peppers, and egg and season to taste with celery salt and pepper.

In another bowl, combine the crab, jalapeños, cilantro, tomato, vinegar, and mayonnaise and mix well. Season with celery salt and pepper to taste. Set aside.

Heat a nonstick pan and spray with vegetable oil. Take a heaping teaspoon of the vermicelli mixture and flatten like a pancake. Fry until lightly browned on both sides. Remove to a cookie sheet and keep warm in a 275°F oven until all are done.

Put a tablespoon of the crab mixture on each noodle round and serve.

Each serving provides
54 calories   3.7 g protein   7.1 g carbohydrate   1.1 g fat
0.6 g dietary fiber   48 mg sodium   22 mg cholesterol

BRUSCHETTA WITH CORN AND BLACK BEANS

Makes 18 appetizers.

Serve this with the bean mixture already spooned on slices of the toasted bread or arrange the toasted bread around a bowl of the bean mixture, so everyone can fix their own bruschetta.

2 tablespoons pine nuts	3 tablespoons balsamic vinegar
¾ cup canned small black beans, rinsed and drained	1½ tablespoons virgin olive oil Salt and freshly ground pepper to taste
1 small tomato, seeded and finely diced	1 baguette cut into 18 diagonal slices, grilled, toasted, or broiled
⅓ cup corn kernels	
¼ cup finely diced red onion	
3 tablespoons finely chopped fresh tarragon	

Toast the pine nuts by putting the nuts into a skillet and shaking over medium heat until they begin to turn golden.

Put the pine nuts along with all the remaining ingredients, except the baguette, into a bowl and toss together. Taste to adjust seasoning. Cover and refrigerate until ready to use. (Can be refrigerated overnight if necessary.)

Serve on toasted baguette slices.

Each serving provides
132 calories   4.1 g protein   21.5 g carbohydrate   2.7 g fat
1.3 g dietary fiber   204 mg sodium   0 mg cholesterol

CHILI-CORN TORTA

Makes 12 servings.

Serve a salad with this great appetizer and you have a delicious lunch or light dinner.

Vegetable oil spray
1 fresh Anaheim chili, seeded and minced
1 fresh jalapeño, seeded and minced
½ cup chopped onion
1 cup chopped celery
1 tablespoon olive oil

1 cup shredded carrot
2 cups corn kernels, drained if canned
¾ cup egg substitute
2 tablespoons Parmesan cheese
Salt and freshly ground pepper to taste

Preheat oven to 375°F. Spray a 9-inch pie pan with vegetable oil and set aside.

Sauté the chili, jalapeño, onion, and celery in the olive oil until the onion softens. Remove from heat. Stir in the carrot, corn, egg substitute, and cheese. Season with salt and pepper to taste. Spoon into the prepared pan and bake uncovered for 20 minutes or until golden.

Each serving provides
55 calories   2.7 g protein   9.4 g carbohydrate   1.3 g fat
1.4 g dietary fiber   45 mg sodium   1 mg cholesterol

WONTON CUPS WITH CONFETTI CRAB

Makes 12 large or 24 small servings.

These edible, easy-to-make cups can be served with all kinds of fillings, such as garlicky chicken or tuna salad, for a quick appetizer—use your imagination!

12 wontons (for mini cups
   you will need 24 wontons)
   Olive oil or water in a
   spray bottle
12 ounces crabmeat, cooked
 3 green onions, thinly sliced
 1 red bell pepper, minced
 2 celery stalks, minced

 1 carrot, shredded
 2 tablespoons rice vinegar
 1 tablespoon lowfat
   mayonnaise
 2 tablespoons nonfat sour
   cream
   Lemon pepper and salt to
   taste

Preheat oven to 350°F.

Take a muffin tin and press a wonton into each muffin cup. If a little sticks up over the top that is OK. Lightly spray with olive oil or water. Put into the oven and let the cups cook until lightly browned, about 10 to 15 minutes. Remove from the oven and let cool.

Toss together the crab, onion, pepper, celery, and carrot in a small bowl. In another small bowl, mix together the vinegar, mayonnaise, and sour cream and season to taste with lemon pepper and salt. Blend this into the crab mixture and spoon some into each wonton cup.

Each serving (one wonton cup) provides
70 calories   7.1 g protein   8 g carbohydrate   1.1 g fat
0.7 g dietary fiber   112 mg sodium   29 mg cholesterol

RICE AND CANADIAN BACON SQUARES

Makes about 12 servings.

Use leftover rice to make this savory appetizer.

3 cups cooked rice
1 tablespoon virgin olive oil
¼ cup chopped green onion
3 cloves garlic, minced
1 tablespoon chopped fresh oregano, or 1 teaspoon dried
½ cup diced Canadian bacon

3 tablespoons lowfat Parmesan cheese
2 eggs or ½ cup egg substitute
Several drops of Tabasco, or to taste
Sea salt and pepper to taste
Vegetable oil spray

Preheat oven to 375°F. Mix all ingredients together and press into an 8 × 8-inch pan that has been sprayed with vegetable oil. Bake for 20 to 25 minutes or until golden on top. Let sit a few minutes and then cut and serve.

Each serving (one rice square) provides
105 calories   4.1 g protein   15.6 g carbohydrate   2.6 g fat
0.3 g dietary fiber   115 mg sodium   40 mg cholesterol

SMOKY PEPPER AND ONION BISCUITS

Makes about 14 small biscuits.

You don't need to serve butter with these biscuits; these little wonders are delicious plain.

1 cup all-purpose flour	1 tablespoon butter
1 cup cake flour	½ cup minced red bell pepper
1 teaspoon salt	¼ cup thinly sliced green onion
4 teaspoons baking powder	½ teaspoon liquid smoke
⅓ cup nonfat cream cheese	1 cup evaporated skim milk

Preheat oven to 425°F.

In a bowl combine the flours, salt, and baking powder. Cut in the cream cheese and butter until the mixture resembles coarse crumbs. Stir in the pepper and onion. Then mix in the liquid smoke and evaporated milk, blending until the mixture just holds together. Do not overmix.

Flour your work surface and pat the dough into a circle about ¾ inch thick. Do not overwork the dough. Using a biscuit cutter, small glass, or cup, cut the biscuits into circles. Push the dough back together and continue until you have used up all the dough. Place the biscuits on a cookie sheet lined with parchment paper. Bake for 8 to 10 minutes or until nicely browned.

Each serving provides

93 calories   4.5 g protein   15.7 g carbohydrate   1.1 g fat
0.5 g dietary fiber   341 mg sodium   5 mg cholesterol

POLENTA AND MUSHROOM CAKES

Makes 4 servings.

Once you try premade polenta, which is available in many deli cases, you will be hooked. It makes all sorts of quick gourmet dishes possible.

2 teaspoons butter	3 green onions, cut in 2-inch
6 ounces *each* chanterelle and	lengths and slivered
portobello mushrooms,	Freshly ground black
stems removed, chopped	pepper and sea salt to taste
½ cup beef broth, defatted	4 (½-inch) slices premade
2 tablespoons white wine	polenta
1 small (about ⅓ cup) tomato,	1 tablespoon chopped parsley
peeled, seeded, and diced	for garnish

Melt the butter in a skillet and add the mushrooms. Cook, stirring, for 2 minutes. Pour in the broth and wine and cook for 3 minutes over medium-high heat. Stir in the tomato and green onion and cook until most of the liquid has evaporated. Season to taste with salt and pepper.

Grill the polenta on a hot grill until lightly browned. Put the polenta on a plate and top with the mushroom mixture. Sprinkle with the parsley.

Each serving provides
87 calories   3.4 g protein   12.9 g carbohydrate   2.5 g fat
2 g dietary fiber   289 mg sodium   6 mg cholesterol

POTSTICKERS WITH THAI SAUCE

Makes 20 potstickers.

To make this a quick and easy appetizer, use the frozen potstickers that are available in most markets. To keep the sodium content down in this recipe, be sure to use low-sodium soy sauce. Lemongrass and fish sauce can be found at well-stocked grocery stores and Asian markets.

20 frozen potstickers	1½ teaspoons sesame oil
¾ cup low-sodium chicken broth, defatted	¼ cup low-sodium chicken broth
	1½ tablespoons low-sodium Thai soy sauce
Thai sauce:	¼ cup fish sauce
1 tablespoon minced onion	2 teaspoons sugar
2 teaspoons grated lemongrass	1 tablespoon rice vinegar

Use a large pot with a tightly fitting lid to cook the potstickers. Put a rack on the bottom of the pan and place the potstickers on the rack. Pour in 1 cup water and cover the pan. Let the potstickers steam until they are thawed, about 3 minutes. Remove the potstickers and the rack and pour out any remaining water from the pot. Pour ¾ cup chicken broth into the pan and add the potstickers. Cover and cook the potstickers until the liquid is gone and the bottoms of the potstickers are lightly browned, about 10 minutes. Remove and serve with the Thai sauce.

To make the sauce, use a nonstick pan and sauté the onion and lemongrass in the sesame oil until the onion just begins to soften. Stir in the ¼ cup broth, soy sauce, fish sauce, sugar, and vinegar and let the mixture simmer for 1 minute.

Each serving provides
65 calories   2.2 g protein   6.7 g carbohydrate   3.2 g fat
0.4 g dietary fiber   555 mg sodium   4 mg cholesterol

DRIED TOMATO AND KALE TART

Makes about 24 servings.

Kale is a beautiful vegetable that is delightful in this easy tart. Try adding it to soups and stews, using it as you would spinach. Phyllo pastry sheets can be found frozen in most supermarkets.

3 tablespoons slivered, dried tomato
1 onion, chopped
2 cups slivered kale
½ cup chicken broth, defatted
1 cup lowfat ricotta
  Salt and pepper to taste

8 sheets phyllo pastry
  Butter-flavored vegetable oil spray
2 tablespoons grated Asiago, or other dry, hard cheese of your choice

Preheat oven to 350°F.

Sauté the dried tomato, onion, and kale in the chicken broth until the liquid has evaporated. Mix in the ricotta cheese and season to taste with salt and pepper.

Spray 2 sheets of phyllo with the vegetable oil. Put phyllo on a cookie sheet lined with parchment paper. Repeat the process, spraying 2 sheets at a time, until you have used all the phyllo. Fold over one inch of the phyllo all around the edges. Fold over once more. Spread the kale mixture over the phyllo and sprinkle with the Asiago cheese. Bake for 20 minutes or until pastry is golden.

Each serving provides
43 calories   2.2 g protein   5.4 g carbohydrate   1.4 g fat
0.4 g dietary fiber   70 mg sodium   4 mg cholesterol

Chapter Two

SOUPS

The following soups are simple to prepare and loaded with robust flavor, especially satisfying on those cold winter nights. This chapter includes hearty chicken and seafood soups as well as superb vegetable soups. When time is really limited, cutting your vegetables (such as carrots, potatoes, and winter squash) into very small dice will help them to cook much faster.

CHICKEN AND RICE SOUP

Makes 6 servings.

Rotisserie chickens from your grocery store give you lots of possibilities for quick meals. Be sure to remove the fatty skin.

1 rotisserie chicken, about 2 pounds
½ cup long grain rice
½ cup chopped onion
1 green bell pepper, chopped
1 teaspoon dried marjoram
⅛ teaspoon saffron or turmeric
6 cups chicken broth, defatted
¼ cup chopped fresh parsley
Salt and pepper to taste

Skin and remove the meat from the chicken. Put the chicken, rice, onion, pepper, marjoram, saffron, broth, and all but 1 tablespoon of the parsley into a soup pot and cook for 20 minutes. Season with salt and pepper and sprinkle with the last tablespoon of parsley just before serving.

Each serving provides

198 calories   21.3 g protein   16.2 g carbohydrate   4.7 g fat
0.7 g dietary fiber   1045 mg sodium   55 mg cholesterol

CHICKEN SOUP
WITH BLACK-EYED PEAS

Makes 6 to 8 servings.

Simmering the broth with the bouquet garni makes a deliciously flavored soup.

2 whole chicken breasts
6 sprigs fresh thyme, or
　1 tablespoon dried
6 sprigs fresh marjoram, or
　1 tablespoon dried
5 peppercorns
3 cloves garlic, peeled
6 cups chicken broth, defatted

1 (15-ounce) can black-eyed
　peas, rinsed and drained
2 tomatoes, peeled, seeded,
　and diced
1 ounce spaghetti, broken
　into 2-inch lengths
3 zucchini, diced
　Salt and pepper to taste

Bone, skin, and dice chicken breasts and set aside.

Make a bouquet garni by putting the thyme, marjoram, peppercorns, and garlic into a cheesecloth bag and tying it up with kitchen twine. Put the chicken, bouquet garni, and broth into a soup pot and cook for 15 minutes.

Remove from heat and discard the bouquet garni. Add the black-eyed peas, tomatoes, and spaghetti and cook for 6 minutes. Add the zucchini and cook until spaghetti is done, about 8 more minutes. Season to taste with salt and pepper.

Each serving provides
247 calories　23.2 g protein　34.7 g carbohydrate　1.6 g fat
5.7 g dietary fiber　1034 mg sodium　34 mg cholesterol

BEAN AND SMOKED TURKEY SOUP

Makes 10 servings.

Ask your deli to cut you a 1-pound slice of smoked turkey. (It is better diced than thinly sliced for this recipe.) This soup is even better the next day.

1 large onion, diced
1 large carrot, peeled and shredded
2 stalks celery, chopped
8 cups chicken broth, defatted
2 (15-ounce) cans white beans, washed and drained

1 (10-ounce) package frozen chopped spinach
½ teaspoon liquid smoke, or to taste
2 zucchini, diced
1 pound smoked turkey, diced
Salt and pepper to taste

Put the onion, carrot, and celery into a soup pot with ¾ cup of the chicken broth and let cook until the broth evaporates. Mash half of the beans and stir into the vegetables. Add the remaining broth, beans, spinach, and liquid smoke and cook for 10 minutes. Add the zucchini and turkey and cook for 10 minutes more. Season to taste with salt and pepper.

Each serving provides
169 calories   16.8 g protein   20.6 g carbohydrate   2.6 g fat
3.9 g dietary fiber   1274 mg sodium   20 mg cholesterol

LOBSTER AND GARLIC CHOWDER

Makes 6 servings.

Flash-frozen lobster pieces, available in many groceries, are wonderful to have on hand to make quick soups (such as this lovely chowder), pastas, quiches, or timbales.

6 cloves garlic, peeled
4 cups chicken broth, defatted
2 ribs celery, chopped
1 shallot, minced
1 carrot, shredded
1 cup potato, peeled and
   diced small

½ cup white wine
1 (8-ounce) bottle clam juice
1 pound frozen lobster pieces,
   cut into bite-size pieces
Salt and pepper to taste
1 (12-ounce) can evaporated
   skim milk

Put the garlic into a small pan with 1½ cups of the chicken broth. Bring to a boil and then turn heat to medium and cook for 20 minutes.

Put the remaining broth and the celery, shallot, carrot, potato, wine, and clam juice into a soup pot and cook until the potatoes are soft, about 15 to 20 minutes.

Purée the garlic mixture and add to the soup pot. Mix to blend and then stir in the lobster. Let the mixture cook for 6 minutes and season to taste with salt and pepper. Stir in the evaporated milk and blend well. Heat the mixture but do not let it come to a boil.

Each serving provides
170 calories   22.8 g protein   16.4 g carbohydrate   0.7 g fat
1 g dietary fiber   1132 mg sodium   57 mg cholesterol

QUICK CIOPPINO

Makes 6 to 8 servings.

Fire-roasted peppers, available in jars in many groceries, enable you to make flavorful soups and sauces easily, such as this gorgeous cioppino.

1 small onion, chopped
2 cloves garlic, minced
2 teaspoons virgin olive oil
1 (12-ounce) jar fire-roasted peppers, drained
6 medium fresh tomatoes, peeled and seeded

1 teaspoon dried thyme leaves
1 (8-ounce) bottle clam juice
1 cup chardonnay
Sea salt and pepper to taste
2 pounds of a mixture of white fish, shrimp, crab, or scallops

In a large soup pot, sauté the onion and garlic in the oil until the onion is soft. Purée the peppers and tomatoes in a blender or food processor. Add the purée and the thyme, clam juice, and chardonnay to the soup pot. Season with salt and pepper and cook for 5 minutes. Add the white fish and cook 3 minutes more. If using shellfish, add this now and cook until the shellfish is done, about 5 minutes. Serve in big shallow soup bowls so that all the beautiful seafood shows.

Each serving provides
175 calories   23.1 g protein   8.6 g carbohydrate   4.4 g fat
1.8 g dietary fiber   775 mg sodium   99 mg cholesterol

BUTTERNUT SQUASH SOUP WITH ANCHO CHILIES

Makes 8 servings.

Dried ancho chilies add flair to this quick soup.

2 dried ancho chilies
1 leek, white part only, cleaned and diced
1 small onion, diced
1 carrot, cleaned and diced small
8 cups chicken or vegetable broth, defatted

1½ pounds butternut squash
1 (11-ounce) can corn kernels
2 tablespoons tomato paste
   Sea salt and pepper to taste
¼ cup chopped fresh cilantro for garnish

Put the chilies in a small pan and cover with hot water.

Put the leek, onion, carrot and ¾ cup of the broth into a soup pot. Let the vegetables cook until the broth has evaporated.

Peel and seed the squash and cut into ½-inch dice. Add the squash to the soup pot and add the remaining broth, corn, and tomato paste. Let the mixture cook until the squash is tender, about 5 minutes.

Purée the chili and stir into the soup. Season with salt and pepper to taste. Let the soup cook over medium heat for 5 more minutes. Ladle into soup bowls and garnish with the cilantro.

Each serving provides
104 calories   5.3 g protein   22.3 g carbohydrate   0.7 g fat
3.1 g dietary fiber   1134 mg sodium   0 mg cholesterol

WATERCRESS AND POTATO SOUP

Makes 6 servings.

Watercress makes this a beautiful green soup.

2 cups watercress, thickest part of the stem removed
1 pound potatoes, peeled and chopped
3 leeks, white part only, cleaned and thinly sliced

2 quarts chicken or vegetable broth, defatted
Sea salt and pepper to taste
1 cup evaporated skim milk

Wash the watercress thoroughly and set aside. Prepare the potatoes and leeks and put into a soup pot. Add the broth and cook until the vegetables are soft, about 25 minutes. Add the watercress and cook for 10 minutes. Remove mixture from heat and purée in a blender or food processor. Season to taste with salt and pepper and then stir in the evaporated milk. Over low heat, stir until well mixed and soup is hot. Do not let the soup come to a boil after adding the evaporated milk.

Each serving provides
115 calories   8 g protein   21 g carbohydrate   0.2 g fat
1.4 g dietary fiber   1411 mg sodium   2 mg cholesterol

CREAMY CABBAGE AND CORN SOUP

Makes 6 servings.

Grilling the corn is worth the trouble because it adds a wonderful smoky taste to this soup.

3 ears of corn, husks removed and corn cleaned

2 leeks, white part only, cleaned and chopped

6 cups chicken or vegetable broth, defatted

1 small head green cabbage, shredded

2 medium potatoes, peeled and shredded

1 shredded carrot

½ teaspoon hot sauce

1 (12-ounce) can evaporated skim milk

Salt and pepper to taste

Grill the corn until dark grill marks appear and the corn softens slightly, about 8 to 10 minutes. Cut the kernels off the cobs and put into a bowl. Using a spoon, scrape anything left on the cob into the bowl. Set aside.

Put the leeks into a soup pot with ½ cup of the broth and cook until the liquid evaporates. Add the corn, remaining broth, cabbage, potatoes, and carrot and cook about 15 minutes. Just before serving, stir in the hot sauce and evaporated milk, then season to taste with salt and pepper.

Each serving provides

162 calories   10.1 g protein   31.6 g carbohydrate   0.8 g fat
3.9 g dietary fiber   1092 mg sodium   3 mg cholesterol

FRESH TOMATO-DILL SOUP WITH CORN SALSA

Makes 6 servings.

This soup is best in the summer when fresh tomatoes and corn are at their ripest.

1 onion, minced
1 large clove garlic, minced
1½ cups chicken or vegetable broth, defatted
6 large fresh tomatoes, peeled and seeded
2 tablespoons chopped fresh dill

Salt and pepper to taste
1 ear corn
1 jalapeño, minced
¼ cup minced Vidalia onion
2 teaspoons virgin olive oil
1 tablespoon rice vinegar

For the soup, sauté 1 cup of the minced onion and the garlic in ½ cup of the broth until the liquid evaporates. Add the remaining broth, tomatoes, and 1 tablespoon of the fresh dill and cook for 5 minutes. Purée mixture and season to taste with salt and pepper.

For the salsa, steam the ear of corn until it is tender, about 3 minutes. Cut the kernels from the cob and put into a bowl. Add the jalapeño, Vidalia onion, oil, vinegar, and the remaining 1 tablespoon of dill. Season to taste with salt and pepper and serve each bowl of soup with a spoonful of the corn salsa on top.

Each serving provides
74 calories   2.6 g protein   13.6 g carbohydrate   1.7 g fat
1.7 g dietary fiber   275 mg sodium   0 mg cholesterol

Roasted Pepper and Sweet Potato Soup

Makes 4 to 5 servings.

This soup would be a fantastic addition to your holiday meal.

3 leeks, white part only, cleaned and sliced

4½ cups chicken or vegetable broth, defatted

2 sweet potatoes, peeled and shredded

1 (12-ounce) jar fire-roasted peppers

2 teaspoons dried thyme

¼ cup chopped fresh parsley

Salt and pepper to taste

Sauté the leeks in ½ cup of the chicken broth in a heavy soup pot, until all the liquid has evaporated. Add the rest of the broth, sweet potatoes, and peppers and cook until the sweet potatoes are soft, 10 to 15 minutes. Remove from heat and purée in a blender or food processor. Return to the pot and add the thyme and parsley and season to taste with salt and pepper.

Each serving provides

127 calories   4.2 g protein   27.3 g carbohydrate   0.6 g fat
3.4 g dietary fiber   1827 mg sodium   0 mg cholesterol

ASPARAGUS SOUP

Makes 6 to 8 servings.

By using frozen asparagus, you can enjoy this soup all year.

1 medium onion, chopped

6½ cups chicken or vegetable broth, defatted

1 (8-ounce) package frozen asparagus, thawed and chopped

1 large russet potato, peeled and shredded

1 large carrot, shredded

1 (12-ounce) can evaporated skim milk

Sea salt and freshly ground pepper to taste

Put the onion in a stock pot with ½ cup of the broth. Cook until the liquid evaporates. Add the asparagus, potato, carrot, and the remaining broth and cook, covered, over medium-low heat, for 20 minutes, stirring occasionally. Stir in the evaporated milk and warm over low heat. Season to taste with salt and pepper.

Each serving provides

84 calories   6.9 g protein   14.1 g carbohydrate   0.3 g fat
1.2 g dietary fiber   873 mg sodium   2 mg cholesterol

BEET AND APPLE SOUP

Makes 6 servings.

Using canned beets makes this pretty soup fast and easy.

1 medium onion, chopped
2 teaspoons butter
4 cups chicken or vegetable
   broth, defatted
1 (1-pound) can beets,
   chopped, and their juice

1 pound apples, peeled, cored,
   and chopped
¼ teaspoon allspice
¼ cup apple brandy (applejack
   or Calvados)
Salt and pepper to taste

   Sauté the onion and butter in a heavy soup pot until the onion is soft. Add the broth, beets in their juice, apples, and allspice. Cook until the apples are soft. Remove from heat and purée. Stir in the apple brandy and season to taste with salt and pepper.

Each serving provides
113 calories   2.5 g protein   18.7 g carbohydrate   1.6 g fat
2.4 g dietary fiber   881 mg sodium   4 mg cholesterol

VEGETABLE AND BLACK BEAN SOUP

Makes 6 servings.

Dried tomato seasoning makes this broth taste wonderful and is terrific in meat sauces and gravies. It adds a delightful richness without fat. When making this soup, you can substitute any vegetables you have on hand. Beef or chicken cut into small dice would also be great in this quick and wonderful soup for cold winter nights.

6 cups chicken or vegetable broth, defatted
3 tablespoons dried tomato seasoning
½ cup thinly sliced celery
½ cup thinly sliced carrot

1 cup peeled and diced potato
1 (15-ounce) can black beans, rinsed and drained
1 cup diced green beans
½ cup chopped fresh spinach
Salt and pepper to taste

Put the broth into a soup pot with the tomato seasoning, celery, carrot, and potato and cook for 10 minutes. Add the black beans, green beans, and spinach and cook until the potatoes are tender. Season with salt and pepper and serve.

Each serving provides
97 calories   6.5 g protein   18 g carbohydrate   0.3 g fat
1.4 g dietary fiber   1255 mg sodium   0 mg cholesterol

Chapter Three

SALADS

Although salads are usually fast and easy to prepare, dressings that are good tasting and lowfat are a challenge. You'll find that the lowfat dressings in the following recipes add plenty of flavor to enhance the salads. Some use sweeteners (sugar, light corn syrup, honey, molasses, or fruit juice concentrate) to help cut the tartness of the vinegar, instead of lots of oil. Using small amounts of strongly flavored oils such as walnut, sesame, avocado, or chili also intensifies the flavor of the dressings. The chapter begins with some substantial main dish seafood and chicken salads, highlights some unusual grain and potato salads, and finishes with a medley of vegetable salads and slaws. If you don't have all the ingredients listed, have fun and experiment with substitutions. Don't ever hesitate to play around with ingredients—that is how great recipes are created.

Spinach and Shrimp Salad with Raspberry Dressing

Makes 4 main-course servings.

This is a beautiful salad that will really impress guests.

¾ pound large shrimp, peeled and slit down the back (this makes them look fuller)
2 cloves garlic, minced
2 teaspoons olive oil
1 large red or orange bell pepper, julienned
2 green onions, sliced
Salt and pepper to taste

3 tablespoons seedless raspberry jam
½ cup seasoned rice vinegar
2 teaspoons minced fresh mint
2 teaspoons sesame oil
1 pound (about 6 cups) spinach, cleaned and cut into ½-inch strips

Sauté the shrimp and garlic with the olive oil until the shrimp just turn pink. Add the bell pepper and onions and cook 30 seconds more. Season with salt and pepper.

Mix the raspberry jam, vinegar, mint, and sesame oil in a small bowl. Pour the dressing into the pan with the shrimp and cook 30 seconds just to warm. Divide the spinach among plates, making a well in the center of the spinach. Spoon the shrimp and pepper mixture in the center of spinach and drizzle with the warm dressing. Serve immediately.

Each serving provides
229 calories   16.9 g protein   28.2 g carbohydrate   6.2 g fat
2.7 g dietary fiber   1772 mg sodium   105 mg cholesterol

GRILLED SCALLOP SALAD WITH ROASTED PEPPER DRESSING

Makes 4 servings.

When jicama is peeled, it reveals a delicious, crunchy, and sweet interior.

4 cups tender baby greens
1 (6-ounce) jar fire-roasted peppers
2 tablespoons lemon juice
½ cup nonfat sour cream
¼ cup chopped fresh dill
Sea salt and freshly ground pepper to taste

¾ pound small bay scallops
Olive oil spray
1 cup diced jicama
12 dried tomatoes, reconstituted in boiling water, drained, and chopped
1 yellow bell pepper, julienned

Clean the greens and wrap in paper towels or keep refrigerated in spinner until ready to use.

In a blender or food processor, blend the fire-roasted peppers, lemon juice, sour cream, and dill. Season to taste with salt and pepper.

Heat the grill. Mix the scallops with 2 tablespoons of the dressing. Spray a grill wok or another grilling device with olive oil spray and grill the scallops until tender, about 3 to 5 minutes. Do not overcook or the scallops will be tough.

Toss the jicama, tomatoes, bell pepper, and baby greens with the remaining dressing. Put on a platter and scatter the scallops over the salad.

Each serving provides
183 calories   20.7 g protein   22.5 g carbohydrate   1.4 g fat
4.6 g dietary fiber   755 mg sodium   28 mg cholesterol

GRILLED TUNA SALAD

Makes 4 servings.

Teaming warm and cold ingredients in salads adds interest. You'll really enjoy the taste and beauty of this salad.

Vegetable oil spray
1 pound tuna steak, ¾ inch thick
12 spears of asparagus, broken off about 5 inches from the top
¼ teaspoon Dijon mustard
2 tablespoons nonfat sour cream
½ teaspoon dried tarragon
2 teaspoons lowfat mayonnaise

2 teaspoons capers, drained
1 tablespoon cider vinegar
⅛ teaspoon lemon pepper or more to taste
Kosher salt to taste
4 cups mixed red and green lettuce
2 tomatoes, thinly sliced and quartered

Heat the grill and spray with vegetable oil so the fish won't stick. When the grill is very hot, place the tuna on the grill and cover loosely with foil. Cook the tuna for about 3 minutes, then turn it over, cover again, and cook for another 2 minutes before checking to see if it is done. Tuna is safe to eat when it is still a little pink in the center. When the tuna is done (this depends on your taste and whether you like it slightly undercooked or cooked through), remove to a plate and set aside.

Blanch the asparagus in boiling water until it turns bright green and run it under cold water to cool it.

Blend the mustard, sour cream, tarragon, mayonnaise, capers, and vinegar in a blender. Season to taste with the lemon pepper and kosher salt.

Toss the greens with some of the dressing and divide among four plates, pushing the greens to the side and leaving the center free. Cut the tuna steak into 4 equal pieces and place one piece of tuna in the middle of each plate. Arrange the asparagus and tomato attractively around the greens. Top the tuna with a dab of the dressing.

Each serving provides

202 calories   27.8 g protein   8.1 g carbohydrate   6.8 g fat
2 g dietary fiber   149 mg sodium   42 mg cholesterol

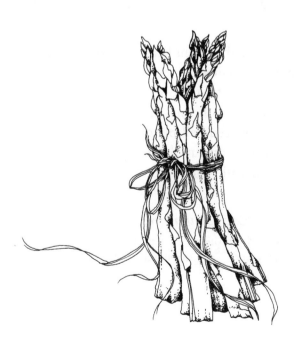

FIVE-BEAN SALAD

Makes 6 to 8 servings.

This salad makes a wonderful vegetarian meal. Cut preparation time in half by substituting one 6-ounce can of sliced green beans for the fresh string beans.

6 ounces fresh green string beans

1 (8¾-ounce) can kidney beans, rinsed and drained

1 (8¾-ounce) can garbanzo beans, rinsed and drained

1 cup black beans, rinsed and drained if canned

1 (8½-ounce) can lima beans, rinsed and drained

1 red bell pepper, finely diced

2 green onions, sliced

3 teaspoons virgin olive oil

⅓ cup cider vinegar

2 teaspoons molasses

Salt and pepper to taste

Cut the ends off of the green beans. Wash and cut into 1-inch lengths. Cook in boiling salted water until tender, about 6 minutes. Strain and rinse in cold water to cool. Drain well.

Toss together the green beans, kidney beans, garbanzo beans, black beans, lima beans, red bell pepper, and green onions. Whisk together the oil, vinegar, and molasses. Pour over the beans and toss. Taste and season with salt and pepper.

Each serving provides

137 calories   6.5 g protein   23.6 g carbohydrate   2.4 g fat
3.5 g dietary fiber   324 mg sodium   0 mg cholesterol

FRESH PEA CONFETTI SALAD

Makes about 8 servings.

I remember my mother and grandmother sitting for hours hulling fresh peas from the garden. If you don't have the time to shell fresh peas, frozen baby peas make an acceptable substitute.

2 pounds fresh peas, shelled (about 2½ cups)

1 large carrot, peeled and finely diced

1 large red bell pepper, finely diced

1 large yellow bell pepper, finely diced

1 cucumber, peeled, seeded, and finely diced

2 tablespoons minced red onion

1 teaspoon sugar

1½ tablespoons corn oil

3 tablespoons balsamic vinegar

Sea salt and freshly ground pepper to taste

Bring some water to a boil in a large pan. Add the peas and blanch for 1 or 2 minutes, depending on how old the peas are. (Older peas take a little longer to blanch.) Drain the peas and rinse under cold water until cool. Put the peas, carrot, peppers, and cucumber in a bowl.

Mix the onion, sugar, oil, and vinegar in a blender. Season with salt and pepper to taste. Blend well and mix with the vegetables. Toss to coat and serve.

Each serving provides
91 calories   3.3 g protein   14 g carbohydrate   2.8 g fat
2.4 g dietary fiber   6 mg sodium   0 mg cholesterol

ORIENTAL CHICKEN DELIGHT SALAD

Makes 4 servings.

The dressing for this salad is almost a salsa, although it has a little more liquid to coat the salad nicely. For quick lowfat dressings, keep a supply of frozen fruit juice in your freezer.

8 cups mixed baby greens
4 half chicken breasts, boned and skinned
1½ cups pineapple juice
1½ cups finely diced fresh pineapple
⅓ cup finely diced red bell pepper

1 fresh jalapeño, minced
¼ cup slivered Thai basil (or substitute regular basil)
2 teaspoons sesame oil
2 tablespoons rice vinegar
Salt and pepper to taste

Wash the greens well, wrap in paper towels, and refrigerate until ready to use.

Poach the chicken breasts in 1 cup water and 1 cup of the pineapple juice until just tender, about 15 minutes. Remove the chicken and, using two forks, shred it while still hot.

Combine the pineapple, red bell pepper, jalapeño, and Thai basil in a bowl and toss lightly. In another small bowl, using a whisk, mix together the sesame oil, rice vinegar, and remaining pineapple juice. Season to taste with salt and pepper. Pour this over the pineapple and pepper mixture and let the flavors blend for at least 10 minutes.

To assemble the salad, mound the greens on 4 plates. Put a mound of the salsa dressing on the top of the salad, reserving about ¼ cup. Arrange chicken strips vertically around the salsa. Sprinkle the remaining dressing around the chicken on each plate.

Each serving provides

250 calories   29.4 g protein   20.3 g carbohydrate   6.1 g fat
3.1 g dietary fiber   101 mg sodium   73 mg cholesterol

Spring Fajita Salad

Makes 4 servings.

When spring arrives and you begin to use your barbecue, this becomes the perfect quick dinner.

3 half chicken breasts, boned and skinned

1 red bell pepper, cored and cut in half

4 slices onion, cut ¼ inch thick

⅓ cup bottled nonfat Italian dressing

4 cups mixed salad greens

2 tablespoons lemon juice

2 tablespoons lowfat mayonnaise

1 tablespoon nonfat sour cream

Salt and pepper to taste

½ cup cooked black beans

12 cherry tomatoes, cut in half

Heat the grill. Rub the chicken, red bell pepper, and onion slices with the Italian dressing. Grill the pepper until it has blackened slightly. Remove it from the grill and put it into a plastic bag and let it sit for 10 minutes (this will help remove the skin).

Grill the chicken, brushing with any remaining Italian dressing, until done. Grill the onion slices until they have grill marks.

Thinly slice the chicken and set aside. Remove the pepper from the plastic bag and scrape the blackened skin with a knife to remove. Cut the pepper into thin strips. Chop up the grilled onion.

Divide the lettuce among 4 plates. Blend the lemon juice, mayonnaise, and sour cream in a medium-size bowl, adding salt and pepper to taste. Toss the chicken, pepper, onion, beans, and tomatoes with the mayonnaise mixture and arrange on top of the lettuce.

Each serving provides

328 calories   44.4 g protein   17.1 g carbohydrate   9.1 g fat
3.7 g dietary fiber   450 mg sodium   115 mg cholesterol

LAMB SALAD WITH
KIWI-MINT DRESSING

Makes 4 to 6 servings.

Use lamb chops for this recipe or a butterflied leg of lamb. You can then cut off part of the leg of lamb to use in this salad and freeze the rest for another quick meal.

1 pound lamb, all fat removed	3 kiwi fruits, peeled and chopped
1 tablespoon garlic paste	1 tablespoon minced mint leaves
Juice of 1 lemon	
Vegetable oil spray	1 tablespoon virgin olive oil
1 cup cooked white beans, if canned, rinsed and drained	Salt and freshly ground pepper to taste
1 red bell pepper, julienned	
2 ounces crumbled feta cheese	

Rub the lamb with the garlic and lemon juice and let it sit for 15 minutes before grilling. When the grill is hot, spray it with vegetable oil, and grill the lamb until it is done to your taste. It usually takes about 5 to 8 minutes per side for medium.

Thinly slice the grilled lamb and combine with the beans, red pepper, and feta cheese.

In a blender, combine the kiwi, mint leaves, and olive oil. Mix with the lamb and season to taste with salt and pepper.

Each serving provides

236 calories   21.5 g protein   15.5 g carbohydrate   10 g fat
2.9 g dietary fiber   150 mg sodium   62 mg cholesterol

COUSCOUS SALAD WITH ORANGE-SESAME DRESSING

Makes 6 servings.

Quick-cooking couscous is handy for side dishes, such as this refreshing salad.

2 cups quick-cooking couscous	½ cup dried cranberries
1¾ cups vegetable stock	½ cup finely diced yellow or orange bell pepper
2 teaspoons sesame oil	⅓ cup slivered fresh basil
½ cup slivered fresh snow peas	½ cup orange juice
	2 teaspoons orange zest

Put the couscous into a bowl. Bring the stock to a boil and then pour over the couscous. Stir in 1 teaspoon of the sesame oil and cover. Let stand for 5 minutes. Remove the cover and fluff the couscous with a fork. Set aside.

Boil some water and put the snow peas in for 30 seconds. Drain and rinse in cold water. Put the couscous, snow peas, cranberries, and peppers into a large bowl and toss together.

In a small bowl, mix the basil, orange juice, orange zest, and the last teaspoon of sesame oil. Pour over the couscous mixture and mix well before serving.

Each serving provides
301 calories   8.6 g protein   61.1 g carbohydrate   2 g fat
2.9 g dietary fiber   8 mg sodium   0 mg cholesterol

RICE AND BLACK BEAN SALAD

Makes 6 to 8 servings.

This delicious salad is made from foods you can stock in your pantry.

1 cup rice
2 cups tomato juice
1 (15-ounce) can black beans, rinsed and drained
2 medium tomatoes, seeded and diced
½ cup chopped green onion
1 fresh jalapeño, seeds removed and minced

1 (4-ounce) jar fire-roasted peppers
½ cup nonfat sour cream
1 tablespoon lowfat mayonnaise
¼ cup chopped cilantro
Kosher salt and freshly ground pepper to taste

Put the rice and tomato juice into a heavy pan, stir to blend, and bring to a boil. Cover and cook until the liquid has been absorbed, 15 to 20 minutes. Fluff the rice with a fork, spread it on a cookie sheet, and put it in the freezer to cool while you make the rest of the salad.

Toss the black beans, tomatoes, green onion, and jalapeño together in a bowl. In a blender or food processor, purée the fire-roasted peppers and then blend the purée with the sour cream and mayonnaise. Stir in the cilantro. Remove the rice from the freezer and add it to the bean mixture. Mix with dressing. Season to taste with salt and pepper.

Each serving provides
174 calories   7 g protein   34.5 g carbohydrate   1.2 g fat
2.8 g dietary fiber   444 mg sodium   1 mg cholesterol

TAHITIAN RICE SALAD

Makes 4 servings.

Serve this salad in a pineapple half for a pretty presentation.

1 tablespoon sliced almonds	2 teaspoons lemon zest
2 cups cooked long grain rice	2 tablespoons dried cherries
½ cup baby peas	¼ cup lemon juice
⅓ cup chopped pineapple, drained if canned	2 tablespoons lowfat coconut milk
¼ cup chopped red bell pepper	1½ tablespoons honey

Toast the almonds by putting them in a nonstick pan and swirling over heat until the almonds become golden. Set aside.

Toss the rice, peas, pineapple, bell pepper, lemon zest, and cherries together. Whisk the lemon juice, coconut milk, and honey together and toss with the rice mixture. Sprinkle a few toasted almonds on each serving.

Each serving provides
197 calories   4.5 g protein   41.4 g carbohydrate   1.2 g fat
1.5 g dietary fiber   21 mg sodium   0 mg cholesterol

POTATO SALAD WITH TOMATO DRESSING

Makes 4 servings.

This is a very satisfying and filling lowfat salad.

1½ pounds small red potatoes
1 medium tomato, peeled
1½ tablespoons dried tomato seasoning
3 tablespoons lowfat mayonnaise
¼ cup tarragon vinegar
1 tablespoon minced fresh tarragon, or 1 teaspoon dried

¼ cup nonfat sour cream
Salt and pepper to taste
⅓ cup chopped sweet pickles
1 cup diced celery (or carrot or bell pepper)

Cut the potatoes into small dice, cover with water, and boil about 10 minutes. Drain and set aside.

Purée the tomato in a blender or food processor. Blend in the dried tomato seasoning, mayonnaise, vinegar, tarragon, and sour cream. Season with salt and pepper.

Put the potatoes, pickles, and celery into a bowl and mix with the tomato dressing.

Each serving provides
73 calories   1.5 g protein   14.2 g carbohydrate   1.4 g fat
2.3 g dietary fiber   93 mg sodium   3 mg cholesterol

SOUTHWESTERN POTATO SALAD

Makes 6 servings.

It's best to use the smallest red potatoes you can find for this savory salad.

2 pounds very small red potatoes

½ teaspoon salt

1 medium jalapeño, seeded and minced

⅓ cup chopped fresh cilantro

¼ cup chopped fresh chives

¼ cup store-bought salsa

⅓ cup nonfat sour cream

¼ to ½ teaspoon cayenne, or to taste

Salt and freshly ground pepper to taste

Put the potatoes into a large pan and cover with water. Add the ½ teaspoon salt. Bring the potatoes to a boil and cook until tender but not soft. Test the potatoes after 8 minutes and continue to cook until done.

Drain the potatoes and rinse under cold water until cool. Drain again and cut the potatoes into quarters. Put the potatoes, jalapeño, cilantro, and chives into a bowl.

Blend together the salsa, sour cream, and cayenne. Season with salt and pepper to taste. Toss with the potatoes and serve.

Each serving provides

176 calories   4.7 g protein   40.1 g carbohydrate   0.2 g fat

2 g dietary fiber   73 mg sodium   0 mg cholesterol

YOUNG GREENS AND GRILLED ASPARAGUS WITH CHILI SALSA

Makes 6 servings.

You can choose any variety of greens that you want. Some suggestions include a combination of baby spinach leaves, small radicchio leaves, watercress, small romaine leaves, tender Bibb leaves, curly young endive, or tender arugula leaves.

6 cups mixed baby greens Vegetable oil spray	2 tablespoons minced onion
3 pounds fresh asparagus, cleaned and broken where tender (about 6 inches from the top)	2 cloves garlic, minced
	2 tablespoons chopped cilantro
3 or 4 fresh serrano chilies	2 teaspoons sesame oil
2 large tomatoes, seeded and finely diced	2 tablespoons rice vinegar Sea salt and freshly ground pepper to taste

Gently wash the greens, pat dry, and refrigerate until ready to use.

Heat the grill and when hot, spray it with the vegetable oil. Grill the asparagus and the serrano chilies. Remove the asparagus when it is a bright green color and slightly tender. If your grill is hot enough, it will leave grill marks on the asparagus. Remove the chilies, keep or discard the seeds (leaving the seeds in will make this salad much spicier), and dice.

Toss together the chilies, tomatoes, onion, garlic, cilantro, sesame oil, and rice vinegar in a bowl. Season to taste with salt and pepper.

Put the greens on a serving platter and place the asparagus on the greens. Spoon the salsa over all and serve.

Each serving provides

75 calories   5.2 g protein   12.3 g carbohydrate   2.2 g fat
3 g dietary fiber   39 mg sodium   0 mg cholesterol

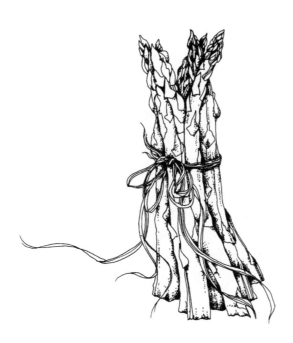

Summer Bounty Salad with Goat Cheese

Makes 6 servings.

Go to your garden or local farmers' market and pick out the most tempting vegetables and greens for this salad.

1 large head romaine lettuce, about 6 cups
1 large cucumber
1 large yellow bell pepper, diced
12 cherry tomatoes
¼ cup minced red onion
4 ounces goat cheese, cut into pieces ¼ inch thick

2 tablespoons raspberry vinegar
2 tablespoons apple juice
1½ tablespoons virgin olive oil
Sea salt and freshly ground pepper to taste

Preheat the broiler.

Wash and tear the lettuce. Cut the cucumber in half lengthwise and then in half again lengthwise (making quarters) and slice thinly.

Toss the lettuce, cucumber, bell pepper, tomatoes, and onion together.

Put the goat cheese on a nonstick cookie pan and broil until the cheese lightly browns. Remove from heat.

Whisk together the vinegar, apple juice, and olive oil and season to taste with salt and pepper. Toss the salad with the vinaigrette and then sprinkle the cheese over the salad.

Each serving provides
124 calories   5.7 g protein   9.7 g carbohydrate   7.9 g fat
3 g dietary fiber   81 mg sodium   9 mg cholesterol

Mushroom Salad with Champagne Vinaigrette

Makes 4 servings.

If fresh chives with their little edible flowers are available, be sure to serve the flowers with this salad. It will look and taste exquisite.

1 head Bibb lettuce, washed and drained
2 cups white button mushrooms, thinly sliced
1 small tomato, seeded and finely diced
⅓ cup minced chives
3 tablespoons champagne vinegar
1 tablespoon virgin olive oil
1 teaspoon sugar
⅛ teaspoon red pepper flakes
   Salt and freshly ground pepper to taste
1 bunch enoki mushrooms

Tear the lettuce and divide it among 4 plates. Put the button mushrooms, tomato, and chives in a bowl and lightly toss. Whisk together the vinegar, oil, sugar, and red pepper flakes. Season with salt and pepper to taste. Reserve 1 tablespoon of the dressing; toss the remainder with the mushroom-tomato mixture. Divide the mushroom-tomato mixture among the 4 plates.

Cut off about ½ inch from the bottom of the bunch of enoki mushrooms. Sprinkle the enoki mushrooms with the last tablespoon of dressing. Make little bunches with the enoki mushrooms and arrange them attractively on the plates. If you have chive flowers, scatter a couple on each plate.

Each serving provides
55 calories   1.8 g protein   5.3 g carbohydrate   3.7 g fat
1.6 g dietary fiber   6 mg sodium   0 mg cholesterol

CHRIS'S SURPRISE CORN SLAW

Makes 6 servings.

Chris Ginty is an inventive and nutrition-conscious cook at a kitchen that feeds the homeless. This is a salad that she threw together one day; it is as pretty to look at as it is delicious.

½ red onion, chopped	2 tablespoons of sweet pickle juice
2 carrots, shredded	
⅓ cup chopped fresh parsley	1 teaspoon dried oregano
2 (11-ounce) cans corn kernels, drained	3 teaspoons virgin olive oil
1 or 2 medium fresh jalapeños, minced	2 tablespoons fresh lemon juice
2 sweet pickles, minced	1 tablespoon sugar
	Salt and pepper to taste

Toss together the onion, carrots, parsley, corn, jalapeños, and pickles. Whisk together the pickle juice, oregano, oil, lemon juice, and sugar and season with salt and pepper to taste. Toss the dressing with the vegetables.

Each serving provides

69 calories   1 g protein   12.1 g carbohydrate   2.5 g fat
1.6 g dietary fiber   134 mg sodium   0 mg cholesterol

FENNEL, CARROT, AND PEPPER SLAW

Makes 4 to 6 servings.

The bright colors of this salad make it very appealing.

1 medium fennel bulb, julienned

½ red bell pepper, julienned

½ yellow bell pepper, julienned

1 small fresh jalapeño, minced

1 large carrot, scraped and julienned

1 cup thinly sliced Napa cabbage

2 tablespoons sugar

1½ tablespoons lowfat mayonnaise

2 tablespoons cider vinegar

½ to 1 teaspoon curry paste

Toss all the vegetables together in a bowl. Whisk together the sugar, mayonnaise, vinegar, and curry paste and mix with the vegetables.

Each serving provides

56 calories   1.1 g protein   11.1 g carbohydrate   1.4 g fat
1.6 g dietary fiber   64 mg sodium   3 mg cholesterol

TACO SALAD WITH
ROASTED-PEPPER SALSA

Makes 4 servings.

Baking, rather than frying, the flour tortillas really cuts down on the fat in this recipe. You can buy taco shell bakers that make large shells like those you get in restaurants, but inverted metal bowls work just as well.

4 large nonfat flour tortillas Vegetable oil spray	½ cup diced red onion ⅓ cup chopped fresh cilantro
3 large tomatoes, diced	Salt and pepper to taste
2 bottled fire-roasted peppers, drained and diced small	12 ounces extra lean ground beef
2 fresh jalapeños, veined, seeded, and minced	1 cup lowfat refried beans 4 to 5 cups of shredded lettuce

Preheat oven to 450°F.

Lightly spray the tortillas with vegetable oil. Dip each tortilla very quickly in hot water. Mold over an upside down metal bowl, or put into a taco shell baker that has been covered with foil. Bake until tortilla is crisp, about 5 to 6 minutes. Remove from oven and carefully remove tortilla. Putting the ruffled side up, return to the oven and bake 2 to 3 minutes more, letting the inside of the tortilla get crisp.

In a bowl, toss together the tomatoes, peppers, jalapeños, onion, and cilantro. Season with salt and pepper to taste. Set aside.

Sauté the ground beef in a nonstick pan until the meat has browned. Season to taste with salt and pepper.

Warm the beans in a microwave or on top of the stove. Divide the beans among the 4 tortilla shells. Sprinkle the meat over each evenly. Put at least 1 cup of lettuce in each shell. Put about ⅓ cup of the salsa on top of each salad and put the rest in an extra dish for those who want it.

Each serving provides
370 calories   28.7 g protein   56.5 g carbohydrate   4.5 g fat
7.1 g dietary fiber   1189 mg sodium   48 mg cholesterol

FRUITY FIESTA SALAD

Makes about 8 servings.

When summer fruit is at its peak, make this refreshing salad.

1 small, fresh pineapple
4 large apricots, washed, pitted, and diced
3 Santa Rosa plums (or your favorite), pitted and diced
4 kiwi fruits, peeled and diced

20 black seedless grapes, cut in half
1 tablespoon pineapple juice concentrate
⅓ cup nonfat sour cream
2 tablespoons marsala wine
Honey to taste

Cut the pineapple in half lengthwise, slicing through the stem so that you have 2 pineapple "boats." Cut out the pineapple fruit and dice it up. Put the diced pineapple in a bowl with the apricots, plums, kiwi, and grapes. Mix the pineapple concentrate, sour cream, wine, and honey together.

Toss the dressing with the fruit and put the fruit back into the pineapple halves to serve.

Each serving provides
108 calories   1.9 g protein   24.7 g carbohydrate   0.8 g fat
3.2 g dietary fiber   10 mg sodium   0 mg cholesterol

GINGERY BEET SALAD

Makes 6 servings.

Grilling baby beets gives them a wonderful flavor. If you puncture the skin of the beets, they will bleed and lose some of their sweetness, so don't cut the greens off too close before grilling.

2 pounds baby beets
Vegetable oil spray

1 bunch red leaf lettuce, washed and torn into pieces

5 green onions, thinly sliced

¼ cup chopped cilantro, and a few sprigs for garnish

2 to 3 teaspoons grated fresh ginger

2 cloves garlic, minced

¾ cup nonfat sour cream

¼ cup orange juice
Kosher salt and freshly ground pepper

Grill the beets on a hot grill sprayed with vegetable oil until the beets are tender, about 4 to 8 minutes if grill is *hot*. Remove the beets and cut in half.

Divide the lettuce among 6 plates. Scatter the beets on the lettuce and sprinkle with the green onion. Whisk together the cilantro, ginger, garlic, sour cream, and orange juice and season with salt and pepper. To keep the tender beets looking good, gently spoon a little mound of dressing on top of each salad and top with a sprig of cilantro.

Each serving provides

96 calories   5.4 g protein   19.8 g carbohydrate   0.5 g fat
1.9 g dietary fiber   137 mg sodium   0 mg cholesterol

Chapter Four

MAIN DISHES

The following recipes are fabulous and substantial. Often, healthful dishes are assumed to have no flavor with portions about the size of a walnut. Not only are these recipes easy, but they are as satisfying and full of tantalizing flavor as some of your favorite trendy restaurant dishes. Good organization and a well-stocked pantry are essential to preparing quick gourmet meals. Go over the pantry section in the introduction so that you have everything available. There is nothing worse than starting a recipe only to find that a basic ingredient is missing. Also, if you have any spare time during the week, dice up some vegetables you know you will be using and keep them in plastic containers with tightly fitting lids. They will last all week, as will cooked rice and boiled potatoes for use in other fast dishes.

BEEF IN A NEST OF VEGETABLES

Makes 4 servings.

If you own a mandolin (a kitchen tool with a blade for slicing and shredding), it makes terrific julienne vegetables. If you don't, just cut the vegetables into very thin stick-shaped pieces 3 to 5 inches long. Broccoli stems are mild and delicious. Save the flowerets for another night.

1 pound top round or sirloin, cut into thin strips
Vegetable oil spray
2 cups beef broth, defatted
1½ teaspoons dried thyme
1 teaspoon sugar
1½ teaspoons freshly ground pepper
2 teaspoons cornstarch mixed with 2 tablespoons water

Salt to taste
1 carrot, peeled and julienned
2 small parsnips, peeled and julienned
3 broccoli stems, peeled and julienned
2 zucchini, julienned

Sauté the beef in a skillet that has been sprayed lightly with vegetable oil. Add the broth, thyme, sugar, and pepper to the pan. Cover and cook on medium heat until the meat is tender, about 15 minutes. Stir the cornstarch-water mixture and salt into the broth. Over low heat, cook, stirring, until slightly thickened.

Meanwhile, steam the vegetables, starting with the carrot, parsnips, and broccoli stems. After 3 minutes, add the zucchini and cook 2 minutes more.

To serve, toss the vegetables together and arrange them in a circle on a large flat soup plate. Mound the meat in the center and ladle a little sauce over the meat. The sauce will flow under the vegetables and give them a delicious flavor.

Each serving provides
375 calories   26.1 g protein   21.6 g carbohydrate   20.9 g fat
3.7 g dietary fiber   506 mg sodium   76 mg cholesterol

SPICY STEAK ROLL

Makes 6 large or 12 small servings.

For a change of pace, you can substitute pork tenderloin for the round steak in this recipe.

1½ pounds round steak, all fat removed and pounded ½ inch thick

1 tablespoon coarse cracked pepper

¼ cup crumbled feta cheese

3 green onions, slivered into 2-inch lengths

1 large finely diced tomato

Juice of 2 oranges

1 tablespoon hoisin sauce

2 to 3 teaspoons honey

1 tablespoon orange zest, or to taste

Salt to taste

6 (2-ounce) lowfat flour tortillas

Heat the grill.

Rub the steak on both sides with the cracked pepper. Grill until meat is done as you like it (about 3 to 4 minutes a side for medium rare). Remove from the grill and slice at a diagonal as thinly as you can (a sharp knife is essential to any good cooking).

Put the sliced meat in a bowl with the feta, green onion, and tomato. In a small cup or bowl, whisk together the orange juice, hoisin sauce, and honey. Mix well and stir in the orange zest and salt and pepper to taste.

Steam the flour tortillas or soften in the microwave. Roll the steak and vegetable mixture up in the tortillas as if they were enchiladas. These are delicious plain or served with a salsa.

Each serving provides

370 calories   31.9 g protein   38.4 g carbohydrate   9.4 g fat
1.6 g dietary fiber   653 mg sodium   80 mg cholesterol

QUICK VEGETABLES AND BEEF

Makes 4 servings.

For a change of pace, try chicken or pork instead of beef in this recipe.

1 pound round steak, thinly sliced	2 teaspoons cornstarch
1½ cups beef broth, defatted	2 cups cut broccoli flowerets
2 tablespoons red wine vinegar	1 large carrot, peeled and thinly sliced diagonally
2 tablespoons low-sodium soy sauce	1 stalk celery, thinly sliced diagonally
1 teaspoon sugar	1 onion, cut into thin wedges

Sauté the meat in a nonstick wok until most of the pink is gone, 2 to 3 minutes. Remove the meat and set aside.

Mix 1 cup of the broth, the vinegar, soy sauce, sugar, and cornstarch together. Set aside.

Put the broccoli, carrot, celery, and onion into the wok and add the remaining ½ cup beef broth. Cover and let cook for 2 minutes. Remove cover, toss the vegetables and cook 2 more minutes uncovered. Return the meat to the wok. Cook 2 more minutes, tossing vegetables and meat a few times. Pour in the soy sauce mixture and blend with the vegetable-meat mixture. Cook for 1 or 2 more minutes or until mixture has slightly thickened and vegetables are just tender.

Each serving provides
244 calories   29.7 g protein   14.9 g carbohydrate   7.4 g fat
3.5 g dietary fiber   780 mg sodium   68 mg cholesterol

VEAL SCALLOPS IN A ROSEMARY-CABERNET-ORANGE SAUCE

Makes 4 servings.

The tenderness of delicate veal scallops is deliciously comple-
mented by this light sauce of oranges and cabernet wine. Serve
over thin noodles or with garlicky mashed potatoes.

4 boneless veal cutlets, about 4 ounces each	1 tablespoon chopped fresh rosemary, or 1 teaspoon dried
¼ cup all-purpose flour	¾ cup beef stock, defatted
2 teaspoons butter	½ cup cabernet wine
¾ cup thinly sliced mushrooms	Salt and freshly ground pepper to taste
Juice of 1 orange	
1 tablespoon orange zest	

Place the cutlets between two pieces of wax paper and pound
⅛ to ¼ inch thick.

Sprinkle the flour on a plate and lightly dredge the veal scallops in flour.

Heat a skillet until very hot. Add the butter and when
melted, sear the veal very quickly for about 1 minute on each side.
Remove the meat from the pan. Add the mushrooms to the pan
and sauté for about 3 minutes on low heat, stirring frequently.
Add the orange juice, zest, rosemary, stock, and wine and cook
over medium heat for 5 minutes. Return the meat to the pan and
let the mixture warm up. Add salt and pepper to taste.

Each serving provides

264 calories   30.6 g protein   8.7 g carbohydrate   9.9 g fat
0.5 g dietary fiber   249 mg sodium   101 mg cholesterol

GRILLED VEAL CHOPS
WITH LEMON RICE

Makes 4 servings.

Lemon thyme is very easy to grow and has a lovely fragrance. Plain thyme can be substituted for the lemon thyme in the recipe below.

4 veal chops (about 5 ounces each, counting the bone)
Olive oil spray
3 tablespoons chopped fresh lemon thyme
¾ cup fresh lemon juice
1 cup long grain rice
1 medium onion, chopped

1¾ cups chicken broth, defatted
Zest of 1 lemon
2 tablespoons chopped fresh parsley
Salt and freshly ground pepper to taste

Heat the grill.

Spray the chops with the olive oil spray and rub with 2 table-spoons of the lemon thyme. Put the chops into a bowl and pour ¼ cup of the lemon juice over the meat. Let sit while you prepare the rice.

Put the onion and ¼ cup of the chicken broth into a 2-quart pan and cook the onion until the broth evaporates. Add the rice, remaining ½ cup lemon juice, 1½ cups broth, the remaining 1 tablespoon of the lemon thyme, and zest. Cook the rice, covered, until the liquid has evaporated, 15 to 20 minutes. Fluff the rice and stir in the fresh parsley.

Meanwhile, grill the meat until it is as done as you like it, about 5 to 8 minutes a side, and serve with the rice. Add salt and pepper to taste.

Each serving provides
410 calories   35.6 g protein   44.5 g carbohydrate   9 g fat
1.2 g dietary fiber   513 mg sodium   114 mg cholesterol

LAMB MEDALLIONS WITH PORTOBELLO MUSHROOMS

Makes 4 servings.

When buying lamb, look for bright pink meat with a creamy white fat. The older the lamb, the darker the meat and the tougher and stronger tasting it will be (used for a stew, this darker meat would be great). Grilling enhances the beautiful flavor of this simple dish.

1 pound lean lamb, from the loin or saddle
Juice of 1 lemon
3 cloves garlic, chopped
1 tablespoon chopped fresh rosemary, or 1 teaspoon dried
Sea salt and freshly ground pepper to taste

2 to 3 large portobello mushrooms
Olive oil spray
1 tablespoon chopped fresh thyme, or 1 teaspoon dried

Cut the lamb into 4 medallions, removing any visible fat. Rub the lamb with the lemon juice. Mix together the garlic, rosemary, and some sea salt and ground pepper. Rub the meat with this mixture and let sit while the grill heats.

Stem the mushrooms and clean. Pat dry and spray with olive oil. Sprinkle with salt, pepper, and thyme.

When the grill is hot, spray it with olive oil and grill the medallions until browned on the outside and pinkish on the inside, 3 to 5 minutes a side. When you turn the meat, add the mushrooms and grill them until they soften.

Thickly slice the mushrooms and place one medallion of lamb with several slices of mushroom on each plate. Garnish each plate with fresh thyme or rosemary.

Each serving provides

201 calories   26.6 g protein   2.9 g carbohydrate   8.7 g fat
0.4 g dietary fiber   66 mg sodium   83 mg cholesterol

GRILLED LAMB CHOPS
WITH AN ORIENTAL SAUCE

Makes 4 servings.

This sauce is also good on pork, veal chops, or steaks.

4 lamb chops, 4½ ounces each
   Vegetable oil spray
2 cloves garlic, minced
1 tablespoon hoisin sauce
2 teaspoons oyster sauce
1 tablespoon low-sodium
   soy sauce

¾ cup apricot nectar
1 tablespoon sugar
2 tablespoons water
   Pinch of five-spice powder

Heat the grill and spray it with the vegetable oil. Cook the chops to desired doneness; when touched with your finger, they will feel spongy for rare, springy for medium, and firm for well-done. With practice you will be able to tell when your meat is cooked to perfection.

Meanwhile, put the garlic, hoisin sauce, oyster sauce, soy sauce, apricot nectar, sugar, water, and five-spice powder together in a pan and cook, stirring, over medium-low heat until sauce slightly thickens. Put the grilled chops in the pan, turn over once so the sauce coats both sides, and serve.

Each serving provides
376 calories   27 g protein   12.6 g carbohydrate   23.8 g fat
0.3 g dietary fiber   512 mg sodium   102 mg cholesterol

VENISON WITH CASSIS SAUCE

Makes 4 servings.

Venison sometimes has a strong flavor. It cries for wonderfully flavored sauces and then shines through. While a guest at Roger Verges in France, I had the most delicious venison with a fruited sauce and some fantastic crusty shredded beets.

½ cup cassis
3 tablespoons balsamic vinegar
1 shallot, minced
½ cup beef broth, defatted
1 cup chicken broth, defatted
1 tablespoon cornstarch

½ cup evaporated skim milk
Kosher salt and freshly ground pepper
Vegetable oil spray
1 pound venison, from the loin, cut into 4 medallions

Preheat oven to 350°F.

Put the cassis, vinegar, and shallot into a saucepan and cook until the mixture reduces by half. Add the beef broth and chicken broth and cook for 2 minutes. Mix the cornstarch into the evaporated milk and add to the sauce. Cook over low heat until the mixture thickens slightly. Season to taste with salt and pepper and set aside.

Heat an ovenproof cast-iron pan on the stovetop until it is very hot. Spray the pan with vegetable oil. Add the venison medallions and cook for 2 minutes. Turn the medallions over and put the pan in the oven until they reach desired doneness, about 2 or 3 more minutes. Pour some sauce on a platter and lay the medallions on the sauce. Pass extra sauce at the table.

Each serving provides
215 calories   29.6 g protein   13.3 g carbohydrate   2.8 g fat
0.1 g dietary fiber   456 mg sodium   98 mg cholesterol

Venison with Wine Sauce

Makes 4 servings.

Venison is very low in fat. Be careful not to overcook the meat so that it stays moist and tender.

2 shallots, chopped
1½ cups chicken broth, defatted
½ cup port
⅓ cup red wine
2 tablespoons dried currants
4 dried apricots

1 teaspoon butter
Salt and pepper to taste
1 pound venison, from the loin, cut into 4 medallions
2 cloves garlic, mashed
Olive oil spray

Put the shallots, broth, port, wine, currants, and apricots into a saucepan and cook for 15 minutes over medium-high heat, so mixture reduces by two-thirds. Remove from heat and strain the sauce. Return the sauce to the pan and cook 5 minutes more. Stir in the butter and season to taste with salt and pepper.

While the sauce is cooking, rub the venison medallions with the garlic. Heat a heavy cast-iron pan and spray with olive oil. When hot, brown the medallions for about 1½ to 2 minutes per side. Ladle some sauce on each plate and top with the medallions.

Each serving provides
228 calories   27.9 g protein   14.6 g carbohydrate   3.8 g fat
1.1 g dietary fiber   442 mg sodium   100 mg cholesterol

Spicy Grilled Pork Tenderloin

Makes 6 servings.

Quick cooking this tenderloin keeps it juicy and tender. You can use prepared Cajun or steak rubbing spices to save even more time, but they are usually very high in sodium content.

1½ pounds pork tenderloin	1 teaspoon sweet paprika
2 teaspoons cayenne	1 teaspoon dried thyme
1 teaspoon black pepper	½ teaspoon salt
½ teaspoon garlic powder	Vegetable oil spray
½ teaspoon onion powder	

Heat the grill.

Trim the tenderloin of all fat and sinew. Cut the tenderloin in half lengthwise, leaving it connected on one side. Press open and flatten the tenderloin with your hand.

Mix the cayenne, black pepper, garlic powder, onion powder, paprika, thyme, and salt together. Rub the meat with this mixture until all is used.

When the grill is very hot, spray it with vegetable oil and grill the tenderloin. It will take 8 to 10 minutes on each side, depending how hot the grill is. When done remove from the grill and slice very thin.

Each serving provides

147 calories   24.7 g protein   1.2 g carbohydrate   4.3 g fat
0.3 g dietary fiber   235 mg sodium   79 mg cholesterol

PORK WITH FIGS AND GRAPES

Makes 6 servings.

Easy and elegant, this dish is perfect for company.

1½ pounds pork tenderloin
2 shallots, chopped
½ cup port
1 cup chicken broth, defatted
½ cup chopped dried figs
1 tablespoon chopped fresh rosemary, or 1 teaspoon dried

Sea salt and freshly ground pepper to taste
Vegetable oil spray
½ cup halved green grapes

Cut the tenderloin into twelve ½-inch medallions.

Put the shallots, port, broth, and figs into a saucepan and boil the mixture until it reduces to ¾ cup of liquid. Strain, discard the figs and shallots, and add the rosemary. Season with salt and pepper to taste.

Heat a cast-iron pan until it is very hot and spray it with vegetable oil. Brown the pork on one side, turn the meat over, add the sauce, and continue to cook until the meat reaches desired doneness. Do not overcook; about 5 to 6 minutes should do it. Add grapes for the last minute of cooking.

Spoon some sauce on each plate and lay 2 medallions on each.

Each serving provides
209 calories   25.6 g protein   14.6 g carbohydrate   4.4 g fat
1.7 g dietary fiber   223 mg sodium   79 mg cholesterol

PORK TENDERLOIN WITH A CRANBERRY-ONION SAUCE

Makes 4 servings.

This sauce is also great on chicken and turkey.

1 pound pork tenderloin	1 cup chopped fresh cran-
2 teaspoons garlic paste	berries, thawed if frozen
1 cup thinly sliced onion	1 tablespoon orange zest
2 teaspoons fresh rosemary	⅓ cup orange juice
¾ cup chicken broth, defatted	Salt and pepper to taste

Heat the grill or preheat the oven to 425°F.

Cut the tenderloin down the center, butterflying it. Rub the tenderloin with the garlic. Grill the meat for about 8 minutes on each side or bake in the oven for 20 minutes.

Meanwhile, put the onion, rosemary, and broth into a small saucepan and cook, covered, over low heat for 10 minutes. Remove the lid and blend in the cranberries, zest, and juice and season with salt and pepper to taste. Cook, uncovered, over low heat for about 5 minutes.

Thinly slice the pork and serve with the sauce.

Each serving provides

184 calories   25.7 g protein   9.7 g carbohydrate   4.3 g fat
1.8 g dietary fiber   247 mg sodium   79 mg cholesterol

CURRIED PORK TENDERLOIN WITH APPLES AND PEARS

Makes 4 servings.

Curry paste has a strong, hot flavor. Add it little by little until the desired hotness of the dish is reached. It is a great product that can be used in lamb sauces, chicken sauces, soups, or even home-made pasta. Using yellow curry paste for this recipe makes a yellow sauce, which is very appealing with the apples and chives.

To cut more fat you can substitute nonfat milk mixed with ½ teaspoon coconut extract for the coconut milk.

1 pound pork tenderloin	½ cup peeled and sliced apples
2 teaspoons olive oil	½ cup peeled and sliced pears
¼ cup brown sugar	1 teaspoon cornstarch
1 to 2 teaspoons yellow curry paste	1 tablespoon chopped chives for garnish
¾ cup lowfat coconut milk	
¼ cup apple juice	
4 tablespoons applejack or Calvados	

Cut all fat from the tenderloin and slice into ½-inch rounds. Sauté in the olive oil until browned, then remove to a plate and set aside.

To the same pan, add the brown sugar, curry paste, ½ cup of the coconut milk, apple juice, 3 tablespoons of the applejack, and the apples and pears. Stir and blend well. Cook 2 minutes. Return the meat to the pan and cook for 5 minutes or until the meat is done. Remove the meat and cooked fruit to a warm platter. Mix the cornstarch with the remaining ¼ cup coconut milk and 1 tablespoon applejack and stir until smooth. Remove the sauce from the heat and stir the cornstarch mixture into the sauce. Return to heat and cook on low for about 30 seconds until thickened. Spoon the sauce on top of the meat and fruit and garnish with the chives.

Each serving provides
321 calories   24.9 g protein   31.6 g carbohydrate   6.9 g fat
1.7 g dietary fiber   89 mg sodium   79 mg cholesterol

CHILI-SPICED PORK

Makes 4 to 6 servings.

This spicy pork tenderloin—lean, tender, and quick cooking—might become a favorite in your household.

1½ pounds pork tenderloin, all visible fat removed	2 to 3 serrano chili peppers, minced
1 tablespoon garlic paste	1 cup chicken broth, defatted
2 teaspoons dried oregano	½ cup evaporated skim milk
Freshly ground pepper	Salt and freshly ground pepper to taste
2 cloves garlic, chopped	
1 small onion, chopped	
1 (6-ounce) jar fire-roasted peppers	

Preheat oven to 425°F.

Cut the tenderloin lengthwise down the center; it will cook faster this way. Rub the garlic paste, oregano, and freshly ground pepper on the tenderloin. Put the tenderloin on a rack in a rimmed cookie sheet and bake for 20 minutes, or until it reaches desired doneness.

While the meat is cooking, put the chopped garlic, onion, roasted peppers, chili peppers, and broth into a saucepan. Simmer this mixture for about 15 minutes. Remove from heat, stir in the evaporated milk, and season to taste with salt and pepper. Before serving, warm the sauce over low heat—do not let boil.

To serve, pour some sauce on a platter. Thinly slice the meat and place on top of the sauce. Serve with extra sauce.

Each serving provides
170 calories   25.1 g protein   7.7 g carbohydrate   4 g fat
0.9 g dietary fiber   622 mg sodium   73 mg cholesterol

SPICY CHICKEN AND PEARS

Makes 6 servings.

Although flavored oils can be purchased, it also is very easy to make your own, such as the chili oil used in this recipe. If you do not use flavored oils very often, make a small bottle, keep it refrigerated, and use within a few weeks. Put corn or olive oil into a bottle and add red pepper flakes, whole peppercorns, and 6 to 12 small dried red chili peppers (2 teaspoons hot paprika is optional).

Vegetable oil spray
6 half chicken breasts, boned and skinned
¾ cup chicken broth, defatted
1 tablespoon brown sugar
2 cloves garlic, minced
1 tablespoon cider vinegar
2 teaspoons low-sodium soy sauce
1 teaspoon ground ginger
2 Bartlett pears, peeled and cut into ½-inch slices
¼ teaspoon chili oil, or to taste

Heat a cast-iron pan until it is very hot. Spray with vegetable oil and brown the chicken breasts. This will take about 4 minutes. Turn the heat down and add the broth, sugar, garlic, vinegar, soy sauce, and ginger. Cook, covered, for 10 minutes. Remove the cover and add the pears and cook 2 to 3 minutes more, or until pears soften slightly. Add chili oil to taste.

Each serving provides
180 calories   27.9 g protein   11.8 g carbohydrate   2 g fat
1.5 g dietary fiber   270 mg sodium   68 mg cholesterol

POLENTA WITH CHICKEN AND WILD MUSHROOMS

Makes 4 servings.

Premade polenta is so handy. It is delicious with this savory mushroom topping, but also try it fried with maple syrup on it, or with just about any topping of meat, beans or vegetables made with a sauce.

1 (1-pound) package premade polenta
Olive oil spray
2 whole chicken breasts, boned, skinned, and diced
4 ounces wild mushrooms, sliced (shiitake, porcini, chanterelle, morels, or a mixture of these)

5 sprigs fresh thyme, extra for garnish
1 cup chicken broth, defatted
2 tablespoons dry sherry
⅓ cup sliced green onions
⅓ cup evaporated skim milk mixed with 1½ tablespoons cornstarch
Salt and pepper to taste

Flatten the polenta about ¾ inch thick and cut it into 3 × 3-inch squares (if you have the kind you slice, slice it about ¾ inch thick). Spray the polenta with the olive oil and broil until lightly browned.

While the polenta is browning, sauté the chicken in a saucepan sprayed with the olive oil until all the pink is gone. Add the mushrooms, thyme, and broth and cook for 3 minutes. Remove from heat and stir in the sherry, green onions, and evaporated milk-cornstarch mixture. Blend well and return to very low heat for 1 minute, until mixture thickens. Season to taste with salt and pepper.

Lay a piece of polenta on a plate and spoon some of the mushroom-chicken mixture over the polenta.

Each serving provides
259 calories   32.4 g protein   25 g carbohydrate   1.9 g fat
1.8 g dietary fiber   708 mg sodium   69 mg cholesterol

GRILLED VEGETABLES AND CHICKEN

Makes 4 servings.

This beautiful meal can be cooked and eaten outside in the summer.

Olive oil spray
12 spears asparagus, broken off at the tender point
1 red bell pepper, cut into fourths
8 baby carrots, cleaned and part of the green stem left on
8 small baby beets, scrubbed
½ cup bottled nonfat Catalina dressing
2 tablespoons brown sugar
1 tablespoon low-sodium soy sauce
2 cloves garlic, minced
4 half chicken breasts, boned and skinned

Heat the grill and spray with olive oil. Spray the asparagus, red pepper, carrots, and beets lightly with the olive oil and toss to lightly cover.

Mix the Catalina dressing, brown sugar, soy sauce, and garlic together in a small bowl and stir until the brown sugar has dissolved.

Grill the vegetables and the chicken, brushing the chicken with the sauce every 5 minutes. Small vegetables can be put on skewers; thin vegetables, such as the asparagus, can be laid horizontally on the grill so they won't fall through.

Each serving provides
245 calories   30.2 g protein   23.1 g carbohydrate   3.7 g fat
2.4 g dietary fiber   373 mg sodium   73 mg cholesterol

CURRIED CHICKEN AND VEGETABLES

Makes 4 servings.

This is great served with rice and a tossed green salad.

Vegetable oil spray
3 half chicken breasts, boned, skinned, and diced
1 large onion, diced
1 large carrot, peeled and diced
2 stalks celery, diced

⅓ cup chicken broth, defatted
3 ounces mushrooms, sliced
2 zucchini, sliced
2 tablespoons curry paste
Sea salt and freshly ground pepper to taste

Spray a pan with the vegetable oil and sauté the chicken until it is lightly browned and partially cooked. Remove the chicken from the pan and put the onion, carrot, and celery into the pan. Add 2 tablespoons of the chicken broth, cover, and let cook for 2 minutes. Add the mushrooms, zucchini, and chicken to the pan. Blend the curry paste with the remaining chicken broth. Pour over the vegetables, cover, and cook over low heat for about 10 to 15 minutes, or until the vegetables are soft. Season to taste with salt and pepper.

Each serving provides
145 calories   22.9 g protein   10 g carbohydrate   1.4 g fat
2.6 g dietary fiber   300 mg sodium   51 mg cholesterol

CHICKEN FAJITAS

Makes 4 servings.

Fajitas make a healthful, appetizing, and lowfat meal, if you eliminate the guacamole and cheese. You can serve these with nonfat sour cream and salsa if you like.

3 half chicken breasts, boned and skinned	1 red bell pepper, thinly sliced
¼ cup bottled lowfat Italian dressing	½ cup chicken broth, defatted
4 (2-ounce) lowfat flour tortillas	1 tablespoon low-sodium soy sauce
1 large yellow onion, cut into thin wedges	1 large lemon, cut in half
	1 cup shredded lettuce
	1 large tomato, diced

Marinate the chicken breasts in the dressing while the grill is heating. When the grill is hot, cook the breasts, brushing with the dressing, until done, about 10 minutes. Remove the chicken and slice it very thin.

Wrap the tortillas in parchment paper and steam on low heat.

Heat a cast-iron frying pan until very hot. Add the onion, pepper, and broth and cook until the liquid has evaporated. Add the chicken and the soy sauce to the pan and squeeze the lemon over the chicken and vegetables. Toss mixture to coat everything and make sure the chicken is hot.

Serve the chicken and vegetables with the heated tortillas, lettuce, and tomato, and let everyone make their own fajitas.

Each serving provides

298 calories   24.7 g protein   39.8 g carbohydrate   4.6 g fat
2.7 g dietary fiber   876 mg sodium   56 mg cholesterol

CHICKEN WITH CHIPOTLE SAUCE

Makes 4 servings.

Chipotles are available canned in adobo sauce. You can find them in most large grocery stores in the Mexican food section, or in Hispanic markets.

Vegetable oil spray
4 half chicken breasts, boned and skinned
1 cup white wine
1 cup chicken broth, defatted
1 clove garlic, minced

⅛ teaspoon aniseed
2 teaspoons minced chipotle
2 teaspoons cornstarch
1 cup evaporated skim milk
1 teaspoon butter

Heat a cast-iron skillet until very hot. Spray with vegetable oil and brown the chicken breasts. When the breasts are browned on both sides, remove from the pan.

Put the wine, broth, garlic, and aniseed into the same cast-iron pan and cook over high heat until the mixture reduces to 1½ cups. Stir in the chipotle and return the chicken to the pan. Cover and cook over medium heat until the chicken is done, about 15 minutes. Remove chicken to a warm platter.

Stir the cornstarch into the evaporated milk. Remove the chipotle sauce from the heat and stir in the butter and evaporated milk mixture. Over low heat, warm until the sauce slightly thickens. Pour the sauce over the chicken and serve.

Each serving provides

227 calories   32.1 g protein   9.7 g carbohydrate   4.3 g fat
0.1 g dietary fiber   431 mg sodium   78 mg cholesterol

CHICKEN IN PEPPER SAUCE

Makes 4 servings.

Try using this easy pepper sauce with other dishes, such as fish fillets, vegetable tortas, crab or salmon cakes, polenta, zucchini dishes, pasta, or any kind of savory timbale.

2 teaspoons virgin olive oil
4 half chicken breasts, boned and skinned
4 ounces sliced fresh mushrooms
1 medium leek, white part only, washed thoroughly and sliced

1 (8-ounce) jar bottled fire-roasted peppers, drained and puréed
¼ cup fresh chopped basil
1 cup chicken broth, defatted
Salt and pepper to taste

Put the oil in a hot pan and sauté the breasts until nicely browned. Remove the breasts and set aside.

Put the mushrooms and leek in the pan and sauté until the liquid evaporates. Add the peppers, basil, and broth and blend well. Add the chicken and cook, covered, for about 7 to 10 minutes. After 7 minutes, check to see if the chicken is done (boneless breasts cook fast and will become tough if overcooked) and season with salt and pepper.

Each serving provides
172 calories   28.8 g protein   4.2 g carbohydrate   4 g fat
0.8 g dietary fiber   464 mg sodium   68 mg cholesterol

CHICKEN AND BLACK BEAN CHILI

Makes 4 servings.

Make this savory chili as hot as you like and serve it with a little nonfat sour cream to help tame the heat. It is also pretty sprinkled with fresh chives.

1 small onion, chopped	2 teaspoons chili powder, or to taste
2 cloves garlic, chopped	
Vegetable oil spray	2 cups cooked black beans, if canned, rinsed and drained
1 red bell pepper, chopped	
2 to 3 fresh jalapeño peppers, cored, seeded, and minced	1 (15-ounce) can chopped tomatoes
	½ cup catsup
2 half chicken breasts, boned, skinned, and diced small	⅓ cup chopped fresh cilantro

Put the onion and garlic in a bean pot, which has been sprayed with vegetable oil, and cook for 3 minutes. Add the red pepper, jalapeños, and chicken. Cook, stirring, about 5 minutes. Add the chili powder, beans, tomatoes, and catsup and cook about 15 minutes over medium-low heat, stirring occasionally. Stir in the cilantro and let cook 2 minutes more.

Each serving provides
263 calories   24 g protein   40.3 g carbohydrate   1.9 g fat
6.1 g dietary fiber   585 mg sodium   34 mg cholesterol

CHICKEN AND CHANTERELLES ON FETTUCINE

Makes 4 servings.

You can find this delicious dish in many pasta restaurants today, and now you can make it quickly in your own home.

2 half chicken breasts, skinned but not boned	4 cloves garlic, chopped
½ onion, quartered	1 tablespoon virgin olive oil
8 ounces fettucine	½ cup chicken broth, defatted
8 ounces chanterelle mushrooms, thinly sliced	3 tablespoons slivered fresh basil
12 dried tomatoes, slivered	¼ cup grated Romano cheese for garnish

Put the chicken and onion in a pan and cover with water. Bring to a boil, and cook until the breasts are done, about 15 to 20 minutes. Remove the cooked chicken from the bone and cut lengthwise into strips. Discard the onion and set the chicken aside.

Bring water for the fettucine to a boil and cook the fettucine until al dente, about 8 minutes.

While the fettucine is cooking, put the mushrooms, tomatoes, garlic, and olive oil into a nonstick pan and cook, stirring, until the vegetables soften. Add the broth and cook for 1 minute. Add the cooked fettucine and chicken to the pan and sprinkle with the fresh basil. Toss all ingredients together and garnish with the grated cheese.

Each serving provides

366 calories   25.3 g protein   48.4 g carbohydrate   7.6 g fat
5.1 g dietary fiber   238 mg sodium   42 mg cholesterol

CHICKEN AND ASPARAGUS ON SESAME RICE

Makes 4 servings.

Try using black sesame seeds in this dish for the visual interest they add.

4 half chicken breasts, boned and skinned	1 tablespoon sesame seeds
16 asparagus spears	2 cups chicken broth, defatted
Sesame oil spray	1 tablespoon low-sodium soy sauce
1 medium onion, chopped	
2 cloves garlic, minced	2 teaspoons grated fresh lemongrass
1 cup long-grain rice	

Heat the grill.

Spray the breasts and asparagus lightly with the sesame oil.

Spray a 2-quart pan lightly with the sesame oil. Sauté the onion and garlic until the onion becomes transparent. Add the rice, sesame seeds, broth, soy sauce, and lemongrass. Bring the mixture to a boil, cover, and lower heat. Let cook until all liquid is absorbed, about 15 to 20 minutes.

Meanwhile, grill the chicken and asparagus. The chicken will take about 8 minutes a side; grill the asparagus until it is bright green and tender.

Fluff the rice and serve with the chicken and asparagus.

Each serving provides

377 calories   33.9 g protein   45.9 g carbohydrate   5.8 g fat
1.8 g dietary fiber   718 mg sodium   73 mg cholesterol

CORNISH GAME HENS WITH A BRANDIED CRANBERRY SAUCE

Makes 4 servings.

The following method of flattening the hens is a fast way of preparing them for the skillet, grill, or broiler.

2 Cornish game hens	¼ cup jellied cranberry sauce
Juice of 3 lemons	⅓ cup brown sugar
2 teaspoons dried rosemary	Zest of 1 lemon
Sea salt and pepper to taste	1 tablespoon water
1½ cups chicken broth, defatted	2 tablespoons Grand Marnier

Wash and dry the hens. Cut each in half along the backside only. Turn the hen breast side up and gently push on the breast bone to flatten. Holding the hen flat with one hand, run a skewer above the leg joint to the other side at the same point so that the hen will stay flat during cooking. Rub the hens with the juice of 1 lemon and rub in the rosemary, salt, and pepper.

Put the hens skin side down in a very hot skillet and let the skin turn a golden brown. Turn the hens over and brown the other side. Add the chicken broth to the pan, cover, and cook for 10 minutes or until the meat is almost done. Remove the hens. To the same pan, add the cranberry sauce, sugar, juice of 2 lemons, zest, and 1 tablespoon of water, blend, and return the hens to the pan. Cook for 5 minutes more. Remove the hens, cover with foil, and set aside.

Stir the Grand Marnier into the sauce. Cook, stirring, until the mixture thickens slightly. Cut the hens in half and spoon some sauce over each serving.

Each serving provides

366 calories   42.5 g protein   31.5 g carbohydrate   6.7 g fat
0.2 g dietary fiber   498 mg sodium   36 mg cholesterol

CHICKEN CUTLETS WITH A CREAMY RASPBERRY SAUCE

Makes 6 servings.

Seedless raspberry jam is a versatile condiment; stir it into cookies, cakes, waffles, pancakes, brownies, or muffins. Use it in sauces or as a glaze for ham, pork, or fowl.

2 teaspoons unsalted butter
6 half chicken breasts, boned, skinned, and flattened ¼ inch thick
2 tablespoons chopped onion
2 cloves garlic, minced

½ cup chicken broth, defatted
½ cup seedless raspberry jam
⅓ cup dry white wine
¼ cup nonfat sour cream
3 tablespoons slivered green onion

Melt the butter in a pan and sauté the chicken until nicely browned. Remove the chicken and add the onion and garlic. Pour in ¼ cup of the broth and cook until the broth has evaporated. Add the remaining ¼ cup broth, jam, and wine and cook for 3 minutes. Return the chicken to the pan and cook for 10 minutes. Remove the chicken to a warm platter. Turn the heat off and stir the sour cream and green onions into the sauce, blending until smooth. Turn the heat on low and just warm through. Pour the sauce over the chicken and serve.

Each serving provides
239 calories   27.8 g protein   20.3 g carbohydrate   4.4 g fat
0.3 g dietary fiber   155 mg sodium   77 mg cholesterol

SHRIMP COOKED IN BEER

Makes 4 servings.

Serve this dish with hot, crusty French bread to scoop up all the wonderful sauce. Sit back, peel the shrimp, and enjoy!

4 cloves garlic, chopped	3 bay leaves
1½ teaspoons dried thyme	2 cups beer
1½ teaspoons dried basil	1 (8-ounce) bottle clam juice
1 large green bell pepper, chopped	Salt and pepper to taste
Juice of 2 lemons	1½ pounds jumbo shrimp in their shells
1 to 2 teaspoons red pepper flakes, to taste	

Put the garlic, thyme, basil, bell pepper, lemon juice, pepper flakes, bay leaves, beer, and clam juice into a pan and let cook on high heat, uncovered, for 10 minutes. Season with salt and pepper to taste. Add the shrimp and cook for 5 to 7 minutes more or until the shrimp are pink and firm. Remove the bay leaves. Serve the shrimp in soup bowls with plenty of the sauce.

Each serving provides

136 calories   19.8 g protein   7 g carbohydrate   1.7 g fat
0.7 g dietary fiber   271 mg sodium   141 mg cholesterol

SOUTHWESTERN SCALLOP BROCHETTES

Makes 6 servings.

Scallops are fragile and tend to stick to the grill if not oiled well. Make sure you spray the grill well with vegetable oil, or use an oiled grill basket. Grill baskets are handy for grilling many small things that otherwise might fall into the coals.

1½ pounds large sea scallops
¼ cup lime juice
2 teaspoons vegetable oil
4 cloves garlic, crushed
½ teaspoon ground coriander
2 teaspoons sugar

2 teaspoons crushed red pepper flakes
1 teaspoon cayenne
¼ cup chopped fresh cilantro
Salt to taste

Heat the grill.

Put the scallops into a bowl. Mix together all other ingredients and toss the marinade with the scallops until well coated. Let marinate 15 minutes. Lace the scallops onto skewers and cook for 2 minutes on a grill that has been sprayed well with vegetable oil. Brush the scallops with the marinade and continue cooking, brushing, and turning until done (the scallops will be opaque in the center). Depending on size, they will cook in 4 to 6 minutes.

Each serving provides
105 calories   15.3 g protein   5.5 g carbohydrate   2.3 g fat
0.3 g dietary fiber   146 mg sodium   29 mg cholesterol

FETTUCINE WITH SNAPPER IN AN ORANGE-FENNEL SAUCE

Makes 4 servings.

Juice concentrates add great flavor to sauces and dressings—without adding fat.

6 ounces fettucine
Vegetable oil spray
1 pound snapper fillets
½ orange bell pepper, minced
Lemon pepper and sea salt to taste

½ teaspoon fennel seed
3 tablespoons orange juice concentrate
1 cup evaporated skim milk
1 teaspoon Old Bay seasoning
1 teaspoon butter

Bring a large pot of water to boil and cook the fettucine.

Meanwhile, spray a skillet with vegetable oil, put the snapper in the skillet, and sprinkle with the bell pepper, lemon pepper, salt, and fennel. Mix the orange juice concentrate, milk, and Old Bay seasoning together and pour around the fish. Spread a piece of wax paper with the butter and put over the fish. Cover with a lid and cook at a gentle simmer for 5 to 8 minutes, depending on how big the fillets are. Baste the fish a couple of times while it is cooking. The fish is done when just opaque at the center. Remove the fish and lay on a bed of the fettucine. Spoon the sauce over the fish and fettucine.

Each serving provides
352 calories   33.8 g protein   44 g carbohydrate   3.8 g fat
2.2 g dietary fiber   342 mg sodium   47 mg cholesterol

FISH AND VEGETABLE BROCHETTES

Makes 4 servings.

Brochettes are always very festive and so quick and easy. If you put the fish and vegetables on the same skewer, the vegetables will still be crunchy when the fish is done. If you like your vegetables cooked longer, put the fish on one skewer, thread the vegetables on another, and cook the vegetables a little longer.

12 ounces white fish, such as cod, sea bass, or halibut, about 1 inch thick
3 zucchini, cut into large chunks
1 large onion, cut into wedges
1 large red bell pepper, cut into large chunks

Olive oil spray
3 cloves garlic, minced
2 tablespoons chopped fresh dill
⅓ cup balsamic vinegar
Kosher salt and freshly ground pepper to taste

Heat the grill. Cut fish into 1½-inch chunks.

Put the zucchini, onion, bell pepper, and fish into a bowl. Spray with the olive oil and toss with the garlic. Thread the vegetables and fish on skewers. Put on the hot grill, cover, and cook for 2 minutes. Open the grill and turn the skewers, cover, and grill until vegetables are done and fish flakes. Do not overcook the fish.

Mix together the dill and vinegar and season with salt and pepper. Sprinkle over the fish and vegetables.

Each serving provides
174 calories   18.1 g protein   12.9 g carbohydrate   5.4 g fat
2.1 g dietary fiber   50 mg sodium   51 mg cholesterol

CRAB AND VEGETABLES WITH HORSERADISH SAUCE

Makes 4 servings.

Serve this on pasta or rice.

1 yellow bell pepper, diced
4 green onions, thinly sliced
1 medium carrot, cut in fine matchsticks
4 ounces snow peas, cut diagonally
12 ounces crabmeat
3 ounces nonfat cream cheese

½ cup nonfat milk
1 to 2 teaspoons horseradish sauce, to taste
1 teaspoon Worcestershire sauce
Sea salt and lemon pepper to taste

Put the pepper, onions, carrot, and snow peas into a pan with ⅓ cup water. Bring to a boil and cook until liquid evaporates. Put the vegetables into a bowl with the crabmeat.

Blend the cream cheese, milk, horseradish, and Worcestershire sauce. Put into a nonstick pan and warm the sauce. Add the vegetables and crabmeat and cook over low heat, stirring until warmed through. Season to taste with salt and lemon pepper.

Each serving provides
156 calories   23 g protein   11.4 g carbohydrate   1.8 g fat
2.2 g dietary fiber   407 mg sodium   88 mg cholesterol

GRILLED SEA BASS WITH CRANBERRY SALSA

Makes 4 servings.

You can use any white fish for this deliciously different grilled fish recipe.

4 (3-ounce) sea bass steaks
   Olive oil spray
1 bottled fire-roasted red pepper
1½ cups fresh cranberries, thawed if frozen
1 Anaheim chili, seeded and minced

3 green onions, sliced
3 tablespoons chopped fresh dill
2 tablespoons fresh lemon juice
   Zest of 1 lemon
   Salt and pepper to taste

Heat the grill and spray the fish steaks with the olive oil.

In a food processor, chop the roasted pepper and cranberries. Add the chili, onions, and dill and pulse a few times to mix. Remove to a bowl and stir in the lemon juice and lemon zest. Season to taste with salt and pepper.

When the grill is hot, cook the steaks until the fish flakes easily when tested with a fork; this will take about 10 minutes.

Serve the fish with the salsa.

Each serving provides
111 calories   15.3 g protein   8.5 g carbohydrate   1.9 g fat
2.5 g dietary fiber   116 mg sodium   32 mg cholesterol

LINGUINE WITH LOBSTER

Makes 6 servings.

You can use flash-frozen lobster pieces in this mouthwatering, garlicky linguine.

9 ounces linguine	2 tomatoes, peeled, seeded, and diced
1½ pounds lobster meat, thawed if frozen, chopped	2 teaspoons balsamic vinegar
4 to 6 cloves garlic, chopped (or to taste)	3 tablespoons slivered fresh basil
1 tablespoon virgin olive oil	1 teaspoon dried oregano
2 tablespoons brandy	Sea salt and freshly ground pepper to taste

Bring a large pot of water to boil and cook the linguine. While the linguine is cooking, prepare the lobster as follows.

Sauté the lobster and garlic in the olive oil over medium-low heat for 5 minutes. Remove from heat. Warm the brandy in a small pan or a metal ladle held over an open flame, until the brandy just begins to steam. Pour over the lobster and ignite. Shake the pan carefully until the fire dies. Add the tomatoes, vinegar, 2 tablespoons of the basil, and the oregano. Season with salt and pepper to taste. Simmer the mixture until the flavors have blended, about 2 to 3 minutes.

Drain the cooked linguine and toss with the lobster mixture. Garnish with the remaining tablespoon of basil.

Each serving provides
317 calories   29.2 g protein   37.8 g carbohydrate   3.9 g fat
2.4 g dietary fiber   435 mg sodium   81 mg cholesterol

SALMON IN A LEMONY FENNEL SAUCE

Makes 4 servings.

I first read about butterflying salmon pieces in Marian Morash's *Fish and Vegetable Cookbook* (Alfred Knopf, 1993). It is a wonderful way of making a small piece of fish look like a generous serving size, and it works perfectly in the following recipe.

1½ pounds fresh salmon, in one piece
1 teaspoon sesame oil
1 tablespoon minced onion
Vegetable oil spray
1 tablespoon flour
¼ cup plus 2 tablespoons nonfat milk

2 tablespoons lemon juice
Zest of 1 lemon
¼ cup nonfat sour cream
3 tablespoons minced fennel bulb, blanched
Kosher salt and freshly ground pepper to taste

Preheat the broiler.

Remove the skin and any bones from the salmon. Cut the salmon into four 1-inch-thick slices. Then with a sharp knife, slice lengthwise through the center of each piece, but do not cut all the way through the fillet. Now open the fillet and flatten with your hand until you have 4 thin, attractive salmon fillets. Lightly rub the steaks with the sesame oil and place on a rimmed baking sheet.

To make the sauce: Put the onion in a nonstick pan that has been sprayed with vegetable oil and sauté for 2 minutes. Whisk the flour into the milk and lemon juice and pour over the onions. Over low heat, cook, stirring, until the mixture just begins to thicken. Remove from heat and stir in the zest, sour cream, and fennel, blending well. Season to taste with salt and pepper and warm over low heat just before serving.

Broil the fish, placing the pan 4 inches from the heat, for about 3 minutes or until cooked through. Serve the fish with the sauce.

Each serving provides

364 calories   38.4 g protein   5.4 g carbohydrate   20.1 g fat
0.2 g dietary fiber   108 mg sodium   120 mg cholesterol

SEA BASS WITH
A DRIED CHERRY SALSA

Makes 4 servings.

You can also broil this great sea bass.

2 tablespoons minced onion	1 tablespoon chopped fresh dill
1 clove garlic, minced	1 tablespoon chopped fresh flat leaf parsley
½ cup dried cherries	
⅓ cup diced orange segments	1 teaspoon vegetable oil
¼ cup orange juice	Vegetable oil spray
1 small Anaheim chili, seeded and minced	1 pound sea bass fillets

Put the onion, garlic, cherries, orange segments, juice, chili, dill, and parsley into a bowl and toss well. Sprinkle the 1 teaspoon oil over the mixture and toss again. Set aside.

Heat the grill. When hot, spray the grill with the vegetable oil. Put the fish on the grill and loosely cover with foil. Let the fish grill for about 6 minutes. Turn the fish, cover with foil again, and continue to cook until the fish flakes and is opaque. Depending on the thickness of the fish, it could take a total of 12 to 15 minutes to cook.

Each serving provides

214 calories   21.4 g protein   23.3 g carbohydrate   3.6 g fat
2.4 g dietary fiber   75 mg sodium   43 mg cholesterol

SEARED HALIBUT WITH A RED YOGURT SAUCE

Makes 4 servings.

If you cannot find chervil, rosemary is also delicious with this dish.

1 (6-ounce) jar fire-roasted peppers
1 shallot, minced
Juice of 1 lemon
½ cup clam juice or chicken broth
2 tablespoons chopped fresh chervil, or 2 teaspoons dried

⅓ cup nonfat plain yogurt
Sea salt and freshly ground pepper to taste
Vegetable oil spray
4 (4-ounce) fresh halibut steaks

Purée the peppers and put the peppers, shallot, lemon juice, and clam juice into a small saucepan and cook over low heat for 10 minutes. Stir in the chervil and yogurt and blend well. Season to taste with salt and pepper. When ready to serve, heat the sauce over low heat until just warm.

Heat a cast-iron pan until it is very hot. Spray with a little vegetable oil and add the halibut. Sear the halibut until a nice crust forms. Reduce heat and turn the halibut over. Cook until the halibut is opaque throughout, about 5 to 8 minutes.

To serve, put some sauce on each plate and center a piece of halibut, seared side up, on top of the sauce.

Each serving provides
145 calories   23.8 g protein   5.3 g carbohydrate   2.8 g fat
0.5 g dietary fiber   308 mg sodium   34 mg cholesterol

SHRIMP AND DRIED TOMATO RISOTTO

Makes 6 servings.

Even if you have never attempted a risotto, please give this delicious and easy one a try. Risotto differs from other rice dishes, because you must attend it until it is done. Arborio rice, an Italian short grain rice, is easily found in most grocery stores.

5 cups chicken broth, defatted	½ cup white wine
1 onion, minced	½ pound large raw shrimp, peeled and deveined
3 cloves garlic, minced	⅓ cup chopped flat leaf parsley
2 teaspoons olive oil	3 tablespoons Parmesan cheese
1½ cups arborio rice	
⅓ cup dried tomatoes, slivered	

Put the broth into a small pan and bring it to a boil. Reduce heat and keep hot over low heat.

Put the onion, garlic, and olive oil into a large, heavy pan and cook over medium heat for 1 minute. Add the rice and tomatoes and mix well. Add the wine and cook, stirring, over medium heat until the wine has been absorbed. Add the warm broth ½ cup at a time, cooking and stirring until the broth has been absorbed, before adding more. After about 12 minutes, add the shrimp and continue adding the broth and stirring until it has been absorbed. Continue until the broth is used up and the rice is creamy but not overcooked. Stir in the parsley and Parmesan and serve.

Each serving provides
286 calories   13.7 g protein   47.6 g carbohydrate   3.2 g fat
1.8 g dietary fiber   929 mg sodium   49 mg cholesterol

ORANGE ROUGHY IN A GREEN PEPPERCORN SAUCE

Makes 4 servings.

Mild-flavored orange roughy makes a wonderful canvas for this zesty sauce.

3 tablespoons flour
1½ cups nonfat milk
½ cup white wine
2 tablespoons tiny green peppercorns, drained
  Juice and zest of 1 lemon
1 tablespoon chopped fresh tarragon, or 1 teaspoon dried

Salt and pepper to taste
Vegetable oil spray
4 (4-ounce) fresh orange roughy fillets

Preheat oven to 400°F.

In a saucepan, whisk together the flour and milk until smooth. Stir in the wine and cook over low heat, stirring constantly, until the mixture thickens. Stir in the peppercorns, lemon juice, zest, and tarragon. Season with salt and pepper. On low heat continue to cook 1 minute to blend flavors.

Spray an ovenproof casserole with vegetable oil and spoon in ½ cup of the sauce. Lay the fillets on the sauce. Pour the remaining sauce over the fish, cover with foil, and bake 15 to 20 minutes or until fish is opaque and flakes.

Each serving provides
215 calories   20.7 g protein   11.7 g carbohydrate   8.3 g fat
0.4 g dietary fiber   229 mg sodium   24 mg cholesterol

HALIBUT WITH CITRUS SALSA

Makes 4 servings.

While staying with friends in Italy, I was served blood oranges with virgin olive oil as a salad course. It was so delicious that now I combine citrus and virgin olive oil in salad dressings, sauces, salsas, and relishes.

½ grapefruit, peeled, cut between sections, and diced small

1 small orange, peeled, cut between sections, and diced small

1 lemon, peeled, cut between sections, and diced small

Zest of 1 lime

½ small red onion, diced

1 tablespoon virgin olive oil

2 tablespoons chopped fresh tarragon, or 2 teaspoons dried

Salt and freshly ground pepper to taste

Vegetable oil spray

4 (4-ounce) halibut steaks, about ¾ inch thick

Heat the broiler.

Combine the grapefruit, orange, lemon, lime zest, onion, olive oil, and tarragon. Season with salt and pepper to taste. Toss lightly and set aside.

Spray a broiler-proof baking dish with vegetable oil. Place the fish steaks in the dish and sprinkle with pepper and salt. Place the pan about 3 inches from the broiler and cook the steaks for 5 to 8 minutes, or until the fish flakes and is opaque in color. Remove from heat and serve with the citrus salsa. The halibut can also be grilled.

Each serving provides
172 calories   22.4 g protein   7.3 g carbohydrate   5.9 g fat
1.1 g dietary fiber   57 mg sodium   33 mg cholesterol

ISLAND SHRIMP

Makes 4 servings.

Dried tomato seasoning (sometimes called tomato splash) adds life to many dishes. It is great sprinkled on pizza, focaccia, salad dressings, cooked in homemade breads, soups, vegetables, or breakfast egg dishes, or used in sauces for meats or pasta dishes.

1 pound large shrimp, shelled and deveined
3 cloves garlic, minced
2 teaspoons olive oil
1 yellow or green bell pepper, slivered
3 teaspoons dried tomato seasoning

½ cup lowfat coconut milk
2 tablespoons oyster sauce
1½ tablespoons low-sodium soy sauce
Salt to taste (optional)

In a nonstick pan, sauté the shrimp and garlic in the oil until shrimp just turn pink. Remove the shrimp and set aside. In the same pan, add the pepper and the dried tomato seasoning and cook for 2 minutes. Add the coconut milk, oyster sauce, and soy sauce and return the shrimp to the pan and cook for about 2 more minutes. Taste and add salt if needed.

Each serving provides
177 calories   21.3 g protein   9.7 g carbohydrate   4.3 g fat
1.4 g dietary fiber   666 mg sodium   141 mg cholesterol

MEDITERRANEAN FRITTATA

Makes 4 servings.

This frittata makes a quick and easy meal. Frittatas are delicious with such a wide range of ingredients that you can substitute almost anything you have on hand.

2 tablespoons minced onion
2 cloves garlic, minced
  Vegetable oil spray
1 Japanese eggplant, quartered lengthwise and thinly sliced
1 small zucchini, quartered lengthwise and thinly sliced
½ cup chopped canned artichoke hearts
1 tablespoon dried tomato seasoning

2 tablespoons slivered fresh basil
¼ cup lowfat ricotta
4 large eggs or 1 cup egg substitute
1 teaspoon freshly ground pepper
  Salt to taste

Put the onion and garlic into a large nonstick frying pan that has been sprayed with vegetable oil, and cook until the onion softens. Add the eggplant and zucchini and cook for 1 minute. If any liquid accumulates, discard the liquid. Put the mixture into a bowl and add the artichoke hearts, tomato seasoning, and basil and stir to blend. Sprinkle the ricotta cheese over all. Whisk the eggs, pepper, and salt together and pour over the entire mixture, stirring to mix.

Heat the frying pan over high heat and spray again with vegetable oil. Spoon the entire mixture into the pan and reduce heat to medium, letting the mixture cook while pulling the edges away from the pan to let the runny egg cook. When the frittata is firm on the bottom, about 3 minutes, flip it over and cook the top for 2 to 3 minutes more. Serve hot or warm.

Each serving provides
129 calories   9.9 g protein   8.4 g carbohydrate   6.5 g fat
1.3 g dietary fiber   97 mg sodium   218 mg cholesterol

VEGETABLE CHILI

Makes 6 to 8 servings.

This tasty and quick vegetarian chili is made easy by starting with canned beans.

1 onion, chopped
1 green bell pepper, chopped
1 cup diced zucchini
½ cup diced carrot
1 (4-ounce) can diced jalapeño chilies, drained
2 (15-ounce) cans western-style beans

⅓ cup catsup
1 teaspoon cumin
1 teaspoon Worcestershire sauce
½ to 1 teaspoon chili powder, or to taste

Put the onion, pepper, zucchini, and carrot into a heavy Dutch oven and add ½ cup water. Cover and let the vegetables cook over low heat for 5 minutes. Add all the other ingredients to the pan and stir to blend. Cover, and over low heat, cook the mixture for 10 to 15 minutes, stirring often.

Each serving provides

141 calories   5.9 g protein   24.4 g carbohydrate   2.3 g fat
6.3 g dietary fiber   748 mg sodium   2 mg cholesterol

SPAGHETTI WITH ROASTED VEGETABLE SAUCE

Makes 4 servings.

Roasted vegetables are also terrific in soups. To make this sauce quickly, chop the vegetables before roasting.

3 tomatoes, peeled, seeded, and chopped
3 shallots, chopped
3 large cloves garlic, peeled
1 carrot, chopped
Sea salt and freshly ground pepper

1⅓ cups beef broth, defatted
8 ounces spaghetti
½ cup slivered fresh basil
2 tablespoons grated pecorino cheese

Preheat oven to 375°F.

Put the tomatoes, shallots, garlic, and carrot into an 8-inch-square pan and sprinkle with salt and pepper. Pour in 1 cup of the broth and bake for 20 minutes. Remove from oven and put the roasted vegetables into a blender or food processor with the remaining ⅓ cup beef broth and pulse a few times to blend coarsely.

Cook the spaghetti in boiling water until al dente. Drain and toss with the roasted vegetable sauce and fresh basil. Garnish with the grated cheese.

Each serving provides
276 calories   10.8 g protein   54.2 g carbohydrate   2.1 g fat
4.2 g dietary fiber   331 mg sodium   3 mg cholesterol

SPAGHETTI WITH GREEN SAUCE

Makes 4 to 6 servings.

This fabulous green sauce is barely cooked, so that you can still taste the freshness of the ingredients. Toasted pine nuts or slivered dried tomatoes are nice additions to this recipe.

½ cup parsley
1 cup basil leaves
1 cup fresh spinach
4 green onions, cut into large pieces
1½ cups chicken broth, defatted
12 ounces spaghetti

2 tablespoons nonfat sour cream
½ cup evaporated skim milk
Salt and freshly ground pepper to taste
2 tablespoons shredded Asiago cheese for garnish

Put water on to boil for the spaghetti.

Put the parsley, basil, spinach, and green onions in a food processor and mince all the ingredients with a few pulses of the machine. Remove the mixture and put it into a 2-quart pan. Add the broth and cook, uncovered, over medium heat for 3 minutes.

Start cooking the spaghetti.

Stir the sour cream and evaporated milk into the green sauce and simmer, uncovered, until hot, but be careful not to let the mixture boil. Remove from heat and season to taste with salt and freshly ground pepper.

When the pasta is done, drain and mix with the sauce. Sprinkle with the Asiago cheese and serve.

Each serving provides

479 calories   23.7 g protein   78.6 g carbohydrate   7.5 g fat
5 g dietary fiber   656 mg sodium   21 mg cholesterol

RAVIOLI WITH
WILD MUSHROOM SAUCE

Makes 4 servings.

Lowfat ricotta ravioli can be found in your supermarket in the packaged fresh pasta section.

2 shallots, minced
2 cloves garlic, minced
½ cup port wine
1½ cups beef broth, defatted
½ cup chopped fresh shiitake mushrooms
½ cup chopped fresh porcini mushrooms

2 tablespoons tomato paste
1 teaspoon dried thyme
1 (9-ounce) package lowfat ricotta ravioli
Salt and freshly ground pepper to taste

Put the shallots, garlic, wine, and broth into a pan and let the mixture boil for 15 minutes. Reduce heat and add the mushrooms, tomato paste, and thyme and cook on medium heat for 10 more minutes.

Bring 3 quarts of water to a boil and add the ravioli. Cook until desired doneness is reached.

Season the sauce with salt and pepper and serve over the ravioli.

Each serving provides
211 calories   11.2 g protein   30.4 g carbohydrate   3.8 g fat
2.2 g dietary fiber   620 mg sodium   43 mg cholesterol

RIGATONI WITH TOMATO PESTO

Makes 6 servings.

This beautiful red pesto also can be used on sandwiches and in dips, dressings, and vegetable dishes.

2 tablespoons walnuts	2 tablespoons lowfat
½ cup dried tomatoes	Parmesan cheese
3 cloves garlic, minced	1 tablespoon virgin olive oil
¼ cup chopped fresh basil	Sea salt and freshly ground
1 tablespoon minced fresh	pepper to taste
rosemary, or 1 teaspoon	12 ounces rigatoni
dried	1 cup chicken broth, defatted

Bring a large pot of water to boil.

Toast the walnuts in a nonstick pan by shaking over high heat until you can smell the oil in the walnuts. Set aside to cool.

Reconstitute the dried tomatoes in a little warm water until softened. Drain the tomatoes and place them in a food processor with the walnuts, garlic, basil, rosemary, cheese, and olive oil. Process until well blended. Season to taste with salt and pepper.

Cook the rigatoni until al dente. Mix the pesto into the chicken broth in a small saucepan. Cook until the broth is hot and toss with the rigatoni.

Each serving provides
261 calories   8.8 g protein   46 g carbohydrate   4.3 g fat
4.9 g dietary fiber   192 mg sodium   1 mg cholesterol

Chapter Five

SIDE DISHES

*T*his chapter is full of easy side dishes created to mix and match with the other recipes in this book. Many children shun vegetables, probably because they have been cooked too long in a covered pot, resulting in a dull-colored, mushy product. Cook vegetables quickly, keeping them uncovered, and you will preserve the vitamins and beautiful natural colors.

APRICOT RICE

Makes 6 servings.

This sweet rice dish is fantastic with chicken.

⅔ cup chopped onion
2½ cups chicken broth, defatted
½ cup chopped dried apricots
2 tablespoons pine nuts

1½ cups rice
1 cup apricot nectar
2 tablespoons chopped cilantro
Salt and pepper to taste

Put the onion and ½ cup of the chicken broth in a heavy pan and cook uncovered until the liquid evaporates. Add the apricots, pine nuts, rice, remaining broth, and apricot nectar. Mix well and cook, covered, for 20 minutes. Stir in the cilantro and season with salt and pepper to taste.

Each serving provides
258 calories   6 g protein   54.6 g carbohydrate   2.1 g fat
1.7 g dietary fiber   456 mg sodium   0 mg cholesterol

POTATO-ONION BAKE

Makes 8 servings.

This is a really fast side dish that uses store-bought frozen hash browns. When buying the frozen hash browns, be sure to check the package for fat content. You can buy them with no added fat.

1 small onion, minced
1 (20-ounce) package frozen hash browns
2 tablespoons chopped fresh parsley
3 tablespoons nonfat sour cream

½ cup lowfat cottage cheese
⅔ cup nonfat milk
Sea salt and freshly ground pepper to taste
Vegetable oil spray
⅔ cup grated cheddar cheese

Preheat oven to 400°F.

Toss together the onion, hash browns, and 1 tablespoon of the parsley.

Mix the sour cream, cottage cheese, and skim milk and season with salt and pepper. Spray an 8-inch-square ovenproof pan with vegetable oil. Lay one third of the potatoes in the pan. Cover the potatoes with one third of the sour cream mixture. Layer again with potatoes and sour cream, sprinkle with one third of the cheddar cheese. Layer once more and then sprinkle with the remaining cheese and parsley. Cover and bake for 15 minutes. Remove the cover and turn the oven down to 350°F. Bake 10 minutes more.

Each serving provides

107 calories   5.4 g protein   16.3 g carbohydrate   2.5 g fat
1.3 g dietary fiber   112 mg sodium   7 mg cholesterol

EXTRA-SPECIAL HASH BROWNS

Makes 4 servings.

You can boil russet potatoes and then shred them or you can use frozen hash browns. Read the label on the frozen brands and make sure there is no added fat.

Olive oil spray
1 pound hash browns
2 teaspoons dried chives
1 tablespoon minced green
   bell pepper

Lemon pepper and sea salt
to taste

Spray a nonstick pan with the olive oil spray. Heat the pan and then add the potatoes. Sprinkle on the chives, bell pepper, and lemon pepper. For the first 2 minutes, stir the potatoes around with a wooden spoon. Now start to let them brown. When golden on one side, turn with a spatula and brown the other side. Season to taste with salt.

Each serving provides
100 calories   2 g protein   22.8 g carbohydrate   0.3 g fat
1.7 g dietary fiber   6 mg sodium   0 mg cholesterol

MASHED POTATOES WITH FIRE-ROASTED PEPPERS

Makes 6 to 8 servings.

Everyone loves mashed potatoes. The flavor is easily varied with the addition of sautéed or roasted garlic, leeks, or onions, steamed fennel or celeriac, green onions, parsnips, cauliflower, or cheese. The recipe below is pretty and flavorful.

2½ pounds baking potatoes, peeled and diced small
 1 (4-ounce) jar fire-roasted peppers, puréed
½ cup nonfat milk (approximately)

2 tablespoons nonfat sour cream (approximately)
Salt and freshly ground pepper to taste

Cover the potatoes with water and cook, covered, until tender, about 10 to 15 minutes. Mash or rice the potatoes and combine the potatoes and the roasted pepper purée. Add enough of the milk and sour cream to give the potatoes the smoothness you like. Season to taste with salt and pepper.

Each serving provides
108 calories   2.8 g protein   24.5 g carbohydrate   0.2 g fat
1.8 g dietary fiber   208 mg sodium   0 mg cholesterol

ZUCCHINI, CARROT, AND POTATO PANCAKES

Makes 4 to 6 servings.

Make a smaller version of these pancakes and serve them with a dab of sour cream and caviar to make an easy and savory appetizer.

2 zucchini, shredded
1 large carrot, peeled and shredded
1 large russet potato, peeled and shredded
¼ cup minced onion
1 teaspoon dried oregano

½ teaspoon baking powder
½ cup flour
2 beaten eggs, or ½ cup egg substitute
Sea salt and freshly ground pepper to taste
Vegetable oil spray

Combine the zucchini, carrot, potato, onion, and oregano. Stir in the baking powder, flour, eggs, and salt and pepper.

Heat a skillet, sprayed with vegetable oil, until very hot. Put a couple tablespoons of the zucchini mixture (for each pancake) in the skillet and flatten. Cook four or five at once, browning on both sides. These can be eaten plain, with salsa, or a dab of nonfat sour cream.

Each serving provides
103 calories   4.2 g protein   17.6 g carbohydrate   1.9 g fat
2 g dietary fiber   54 mg sodium   70 mg cholesterol

SAVORY GREENS IN ONION BROTH

Makes 6 to 8 servings.

Slow simmering of onions reveals their sweetness.

2 yellow onions, minced
2½ cups chicken, beef, or vegetable broth
1 tablespoon dried tomato paste (use the type that comes in a tube)

6 cups chopped greens (such as kale, chard, spinach, broccoli rabe, collard greens, or a mixture of these)
Kosher or sea salt and freshly ground pepper to taste

Put the onions, 1½ cups of the broth, and dried tomato into a pan and cook, covered, over medium heat for 20 minutes. Add the remaining 1 cup broth and bring to a boil. Add the greens and cook for 2 to 3 minutes until the greens are tender. Season with salt and pepper to taste.

Each serving provides
34 calories   2.3 g protein   6.6 g carbohydrate   0.3 g fat
1.5 g dietary fiber   343 mg sodium   0 mg cholesterol

SAUTÉED PEARS AND SWEET POTATO WEDGES

Makes 6 servings.

Serve this as a side dish with pork chops, ham, or chicken.

2 small sweet potatoes, peeled and cut into thin wedges
2 Anjou pears, peeled, cored, and cut into thin wedges
⅓ cup brown sugar

¼ cup lemon juice
Zest of 1 lemon
1 teaspoon butter
2 tablespoons brandy

Put the sweet potatoes in a skillet with ½ cup water and let cook, covered, for about 7 minutes. Add the pears, brown sugar, lemon juice, and zest and cook, tossing the mixture, for 3 minutes. Stir in the butter and brandy and let simmer 1 more minute.

Each serving provides

148 calories   1 g protein   32.8 g carbohydrate   1 g fat
2.7 g dietary fiber   18 mg sodium   2 mg cholesterol

SWEET POTATOES WITH CRANBERRIES

Makes 4 to 6 servings.

This delicious and colorful dish would look wonderful on your Thanksgiving table.

1 teaspoon butter
3 cups diced cooked sweet potatoes
1 cup dried cranberries
1 (8-ounce) can crushed pineapple, drained

¼ cup brown sugar
2 tablespoons light corn syrup
½ teaspoon ground cinnamon
⅛ teaspoon nutmeg
⅛ teaspoon ground ginger
2 tablespoons whiskey

Spread the butter in a skillet. Heat the skillet and add the sweet potatoes, cranberries, drained pineapple, sugar, and corn syrup. Toss the ingredients over medium-high heat for about 2 minutes or until the sugar completely melts. Stir in the cinnamon, nutmeg, and ginger and cook for 1 minute more. Stir in the whiskey, cooking 1 more minute.

Each serving provides
249 calories   1.4 g protein   59.4 g carbohydrate   0.4 g fat
3.6 g dietary fiber   23 mg sodium   0 mg cholesterol

GARLICKY CUCUMBER-TOMATO DICE

Makes 4 servings.

Try this cold in the summer and warm in the winter.

1 English cucumber
2 teaspoons virgin olive oil
2 large tomatoes, seeded and diced
3 cloves garlic, minced
2 tablespoons chopped fresh basil, tarragon, or dill

1 tablespoon white wine vinegar
Kosher salt and freshly ground pepper to taste

Cut the ends off the cucumber and slit it lengthwise down the center. Remove the seeds and cut the cucumber into ¼-inch-thick slices.

Heat a nonstick skillet. Add the olive oil, cucumber, tomatoes, and garlic. Toss while cooking for 2 minutes. You just want to heat everything so flavors intensify. Sprinkle with the fresh herb and vinegar and toss, letting everything warm up. Season with salt and pepper and serve.

Each serving provides
44 calories   1 g protein   5.4 g carbohydrate   2.6 g fat
1.4 g dietary fiber   7 mg sodium   0 mg cholesterol

GREENS AND PINE NUTS

Makes 6 servings.

Try cooking healthful greens with other vegetables, in soups, stews, and pasta dishes. The strong flavor of some greens (such as turnip and mustard greens) can be lessened by blanching them in water and draining before cooking. A recipe like this will also cut the bite. Try using collards, broccoli rabe, kale, beet greens, dandelion greens, mustard greens, turnip greens, cabbage, chard, or spinach, or a combination of these.

2 shallots, minced
2 cloves garlic, minced
1 cup vegetable broth
6 cups chopped greens

1 tablespoon pine nuts
Salt and freshly ground
pepper

Put the shallots and garlic in a large skillet with ½ cup of the broth. Over medium-high heat, cook until the liquid has evaporated (be careful not to burn the garlic). Add the remaining broth and the greens and toss so the greens are coated with broth. Cover and cook 2 to 3 minutes. Remove the cover and add the pine nuts, toss, and cook over high heat until the liquid evaporates. Season to taste with salt and freshly ground pepper.

Each serving provides
44 calories   2.7 g protein   7.8 g carbohydrate   1.1 g fat
1.3 g dietary fiber   211 mg sodium   0 mg cholesterol

BAKED ZUCCHINI

Makes 4 servings.

As luscious as fried zucchini but without the fat.

4 zucchini, each cut lengthwise into 4 slices

⅓ cup nonfat bottled Italian
dressing

2½ tablespoons lowfat
Parmesan cheese

2 teaspoons dried oregano
Freshly ground pepper

Preheat the oven to 400°F.

Line up the sliced zucchini in a rimmed cookie sheet. Brush the zucchini with the dressing. Mix together the cheese, oregano, and pepper and sprinkle on each piece of zucchini. Bake until the cheese turns golden and zucchini begins to soften, about 8 to 10 minutes.

Each serving provides

64 calories   2.5 g protein   11.4 g carbohydrate   1.5 g fat
2.6 g dietary fiber   373 mg sodium   4 mg cholesterol

BRAISED FENNEL

Makes 3 to 6 servings.

Fennel is a fantastic vegetable that is great raw, boiled, mashed (with potatoes or alone), grilled, or braised as in this recipe.

1 small onion, chopped
2 cloves garlic, minced
1 medium tomato, peeled, seeded, and chopped
2 cups beef broth, defatted
3 medium fennel bulbs, cut in half

Kosher salt and freshly ground pepper to taste
1 teaspoon butter
1 tablespoon freshly grated Parmesan (or any hard cheese)

Put the onion, garlic, and tomato into a skillet. Add ⅓ cup of the beef broth and let boil until the liquid evaporates. Put the fennel in, cut side down, sprinkle with salt and pepper, and add the remaining beef broth. Cover with wax paper that has been coated with the butter and then tightly cover with a lid or foil on top of the pan. Cook over medium-low heat for 20 to 25 minutes or until tender, basting 2 to 3 times during cooking. Remove the cover and wax paper and turn heat on high to evaporate all liquid. Remove to a warm platter and sprinkle with the cheese.

Each serving provides
57 calories   3 g protein   11.5 g carbohydrate   0.6 g fat
2.5 g dietary fiber   356 mg sodium   1 mg cholesterol

BROCCOLI WITH LEMON-PEPPER CREAM

Makes 4 servings.

A bright and crunchy dish that you and your children will love.

1 pound broccoli
2 cloves garlic, minced
1 tablespoon minced onion
⅓ cup water
2 tablespoons nonfat sour cream

¼ teaspoon sugar
1 tablespoon lowfat mayonnaise
Zest and juice of ½ lemon
Lemon pepper and salt to taste

Cut the broccoli into small flowerets. Peel the stems and cut the stems into thin rounds.

Put the broccoli, garlic, onion, and water into a wok and cook, tossing, for 2 minutes. Cover and cook for 2 minutes more. Uncover and turn the heat to high and let all liquid evaporate.

While the broccoli is cooking, blend the sour cream, sugar, mayonnaise, lemon zest and juice, then season to taste with lemon pepper and salt. Pour the sauce over the broccoli, toss, and serve.

Each serving provides
47 calories   3.5 g protein   7.3 g carbohydrate   1.4 g fat
2.4 g dietary fiber   58 mg sodium   3 mg cholesterol

MEDITERRANEAN EGGPLANT WITH FRESH BASIL

Makes 4 servings.

The smaller, Japanese eggplants work better when you are trying to prepare a dish in a short time. The larger eggplants really need to be salted and drained when using in quick recipes or they become mushy.

1 tablespoon virgin olive oil	⅓ cup chopped fresh basil
4 Japanese eggplants, ends removed, diced	2 tablespoons balsamic vinegar
3 tablespoons onion, chopped	Kosher salt and freshly ground pepper to taste
2 cloves garlic, minced	1 tablespoon grated Parmesan cheese
2 tomatoes, peeled, seeded and diced	

Put the oil in a skillet and heat the skillet until very hot. Add the eggplant, onion, and garlic, tossing and cooking for 2 to 3 minutes or until vegetables soften. Add the tomatoes, basil, and vinegar and toss, cooking 1 more minute. Season to taste with salt and pepper. Sprinkle with Parmesan cheese and serve.

Each serving provides
91 calories   2.5 g protein   12.7 g carbohydrate   4.1 g fat
2.1 g dietary fiber   33 mg sodium   1 mg cholesterol

LEEKS WITH ASIAGO CHEESE

Makes 4 servings.

Braising vegetables in broth gives them a richness usually achieved with lots of butter.

4 medium leeks
Vegetable oil spray
Kosher salt and freshly
ground pepper
1¼ cups chicken or beef broth,
defatted

1 teaspoon butter
1 tablespoon shredded
Asiago cheese

Preheat the broiler.

Trim the root ends off the leeks. Cut off most of the green ends, leaving only about 3 inches of the green. Slit each leek lengthwise and wash to remove any sand and dirt. Spray an oven-proof sauté pan with vegetable oil and then lay the leeks, cut side down, in the pan. Sprinkle the leeks with salt and pepper and pour in the broth to come halfway up the leeks. Cover the leeks with wax paper you have spread with the butter and then cover tightly with a lid. Simmer, basting with the braising liquid several times, for 15 to 20 minutes. When tender, remove the lid and the wax paper and sprinkle with the Asiago cheese. Put the pan under the broiler until the cheese lightly browns.

Each serving provides
61 calories   2.5 g protein   8.1 g carbohydrate   2.3 g fat
0.8 g dietary fiber   365 mg sodium   6 mg cholesterol

MAPLE-GLAZED PARSNIPS AND CARROTS

Makes 6 servings.

Parsnips are sweet and nutty tasting when young and less tender and stronger tasting as they age. They are wonderful in soups and stews or puréed with mashed potatoes.

1 pound parsnips, peeled and julienned
1 pound carrots, peeled and julienned
½ cup water
2 teaspoons butter

¼ cup maple syrup
1 teaspoon ground coriander
¼ teaspoon ground nutmeg
1 tablespoon rum
1 tablespoon fresh chopped mint for garnish

Put the parsnips and carrots into a skillet with the water. Cover and cook for 3 to 5 minutes or until the vegetables soften. Add the butter, maple syrup, coriander, and nutmeg and continue to cook and stir for 2 more minutes. Stir in the rum, cooking 1 to 2 minutes more. Serve garnished with fresh mint.

Each serving provides
128 calories   1.6 g protein   27.5 g carbohydrate   1.7 g fat
2.5 g dietary fiber   64 mg sodium   4 mg cholesterol

GRILLED VEGETABLE PLATTER

Makes about 1/2 cup sauce.

Vegetable platters are healthful and beautiful, but they often taste drab and dull when the vegetables are steamed. Grilling is what makes this platter special.

Select four or five of the following vegetables:
Baby carrots, green onions, baby beets, cauliflower, new potatoes, asparagus, green beans, fennel, baby corn, zucchini, Japanese eggplant, cherry tomatoes, white mushrooms, portobello mushrooms, sweet potato slices, winter squash

⅓ cup bottled lowfat Italian dressing

For the sauce:
⅓ cup nonfat yogurt (strained or not)
2 tablespoons lowfat mayonnaise

Heat the grill. Sprinkle the dressing on the vegetables and then cook on a very hot grill just until there are grill marks. For the sauce, mix the yogurt with the mayonnaise. To this add any of the following:

- Dried tomato seasoning, garlic, salt, and pepper
- 1 jalapeño, 1 tablespoon chopped cilantro, and salt and pepper to taste

- 1 to 2 teaspoons Dijon mustard, ½ teaspoon sugar, 1 tablespoon chopped fresh dill
- 1 teaspoon to 1 tablespoon curry paste (depending on personal preference), celery seed, and 1 tablespoon cider vinegar

Each serving (one tablespoon) provides

19 calories   0.6 g protein   1.2 g carbohydrate   1.3 g fat
0.1 g dietary fiber   37 mg sodium   3 mg cholesterol

Curried Vegetables

Makes 6 servings.

This curry sparks up vegetables and adds interest to a simple meal. You can vary the vegetables according to what is in season or in your garden, pantry, or freezer.

1 large onion, diced
2 cloves garlic, chopped
1 tablespoon virgin olive oil
2 large carrots, diced
1 potato, peeled and diced small
1 red bell pepper, diced

3 zucchini, diced
2/3 cup corn kernels
2 tablespoons curry paste (or to taste) mixed with 2 tablespoons water
Salt and freshly ground pepper to taste

Put the onion, garlic, and oil in a heavy pan and cook, stirring, for 2 minutes. Add the carrots, potato, red pepper, zucchini, corn, and curry mixture and blend well. Cover and, on low heat, cook for 20 minutes, stirring occasionally. The natural juices of the vegetables should keep this from burning if the heat is low enough, but add a little water if necessary. Season to taste with salt and pepper.

Each serving provides
98 calories   2.4 g protein   18.2 g carbohydrate   2.6 g fat
3 g dietary fiber   110 mg sodium   0 mg cholesterol

MEXICAN VEGETABLES

Makes 6 servings.

Try serving this flavorful side dish on top of grilled white fish—it's great.

1 small onion, cut into thin wedges
2 cloves garlic, chopped
Vegetable oil spray
4 zucchini, diced
2 large tomatoes, peeled and chopped

1 cup corn kernels
1 fresh jalapeño, membranes and seeds removed, minced
1 teaspoon dried oregano
¼ cup chopped fresh cilantro
Sea salt and freshly ground pepper to taste

Put the onion and garlic in a skillet that has been sprayed with vegetable oil. Sauté the onions until they become transparent. Add the zucchini, tomatoes, corn, jalapeño, and oregano, then cook over low heat for about 5 minutes or until the zucchini is slightly softened. Stir in the cilantro and season to taste with salt and pepper.

Each serving provides
61 calories   2.2 g protein   14.2 g carbohydrate   0.6 g fat
3.1 g dietary fiber   8 mg sodium   0 mg cholesterol

THAI SPICED VEGETABLES

Makes 4 servings.

This terrific spicy vegetable dish will complement milder chicken or fish dishes.

Vegetable oil spray
1 small onion, cut into thin wedges
2 cloves garlic, slivered
2 carrots, julienned
1 large red bell pepper, julienned
¼ to ½ teaspoon Thai chili paste
1 tablespoon low-sodium soy sauce
1 teaspoon sugar
1 cup julienned snow peas
1 tablespoon oyster sauce
⅓ cup slivered Thai basil or regular basil

Heat a wok until very hot. Spray with the vegetable oil and sauté the onion, garlic, and carrots for 2 minutes. Add the red bell pepper and 2 tablespoons of water and toss, cooking 2 minutes more. Add the chili paste, soy sauce, sugar, snow peas, and oyster sauce. Toss and cook 1 to 2 minutes. Toss with the basil and serve.

Each serving provides
64 calories   2.8 g protein   13.5 g carbohydrate   0.3 g fat
2.5 g dietary fiber   346 mg sodium   0 mg cholesterol

VEGETABLE STIR FRY
WITH COCONUT MILK

Makes 4 to 6 servings.

You can add chicken breast, beef, pork, or shrimp to this dish. If you add three boneless, skinless half chicken breasts to this recipe, dice and sauté the chicken, then set it aside. Cook the vegetables, adding the chicken again when you add the coconut milk. This is great served over rice.

1 small red bell pepper, seeded and slivered

1 large carrot, cut into thin diagonal slices

6 ounces snap peas

1 teaspoon sesame oil

½ cup chicken broth, defatted

1 cup lite coconut milk, mixed with 1 tablespoon cornstarch

3 tablespoons oyster sauce

3 tablespoons low-sodium soy sauce

Chili oil to taste

⅓ cup green onion, cut into thin diagonal slices

Sauté the red pepper, carrot, and peas in the sesame oil and broth until the broth evaporates and the vegetables begin to get tender. Whisk the coconut milk, oyster sauce, soy sauce, and chili oil together until well blended. Add to the vegetables along with the green onions and cook until the sauce begins to thicken.

Each serving provides
72 calories   2.6 g protein   9.3 g carbohydrate   1 g fat
1.2 g dietary fiber   688 mg sodium   0 mg cholesterol

Chapter Six

DESSERTS

*T*his chapter is full of quick and luscious desserts that are perfect to serve to family or company. Perhaps you'll find a favorite among them.

ALOHA FAVORITE

Makes 8 servings.

Substitute your favorite fruits in this refreshing dessert.

2 cups diced fresh pineapple
1 papaya, peeled, seeded, and diced
3 kiwi fruits, peeled and diced
4 figs, peeled and quartered
2 cups diced honeydew melon

2 tablespoons flaked coconut
Dash of amaretto to taste
1 (8-ounce) carton nonfat vanilla yogurt
3 tablespoons lowfat granola

Toss the fruits and coconut together and sprinkle with the amaretto. Spoon into dessert bowls or wine glasses and serve with a spoonful of vanilla yogurt and a sprinkling of granola on each.

Each serving provides
138 calories   3.2 g protein   29.6 g carbohydrate   1.7 g fat
2.8 g dietary fiber   37 mg sodium   1 mg cholesterol

PEACH MOUSSE

Makes 4 servings.

A fast, light, and versatile dessert that can be made with many other fruits. You can also substitute ½ cup freezer jam for the canned fruit. Freezer jam is much fresher tasting than cooked jam and works great in this recipe.

1 (15¼-ounce) can of sliced peaches, drained
1 cup whipped dessert topping

3 ounces nonfat cream cheese
2 tablespoons lowfat sour cream
Pinch of nutmeg

Using a food processor, pulse the drained peaches a few times to mince. Drain again and then fold the peaches into the dessert topping. Blend the cream cheese, sour cream, and nutmeg together. Fold into the peach mixture and spoon into champagne glasses or pretty wine glasses and refrigerate until ready to eat. The mousse can also be put into the freezer, but not for more than 20 minutes, so it stays light and fluffy.

Each serving provides
107 calories   4.1 g protein   12.7 g carbohydrate   4 g fat
0.8 g dietary fiber   135 mg sodium   4 mg cholesterol

PINEAPPLE FOSTER

Makes 4 servings.

A delicious variation of the traditional banana foster. Try making up your own versions using other fresh fruits.

2 teaspoons butter
4 slices fresh pineapple, peeled and cut in half
¼ cup brown sugar

¼ cup dark rum
1 teaspoon cinnamon
1 (8-ounce) carton nonfat vanilla yogurt

Melt the butter in a nonstick pan. Add the pineapple slices and cook about 1 minute. Turn the slices over and add the brown sugar. Shake the pan and cook until the pineapple is hot and beginning to brown slightly. Turn the pineapple over again and add the dark rum. Ignite the rum and let cook until the flames die down. Sprinkle with the cinnamon and serve with a little nonfat vanilla yogurt.

Each serving provides
176 calories   3.6 g protein   29.2 g carbohydrate   2.6 g fat
1.1 g dietary fiber   72 mg sodium   7 mg cholesterol

FLOATING ISLANDS

Makes 4 servings.

These light and lovely islands traditionally float on a sea of custard. Here they are served in a simple and quick blueberry sauce.

¼ cup canned blueberry pie filling
¾ cup whipped, frozen dessert topping, defrosted
3½ cups nonfat milk
½ cup light rum

3 egg whites
¼ teaspoon cream of tartar
2 tablespoons superfine sugar
½ teaspoon cinnamon
¼ teaspoon nutmeg

Mix together the pie filling and dessert topping and refrigerate until ready to use.

Put the milk and rum into a saucepan and, over low heat, bring to a simmer. Meanwhile beat the egg whites and cream of tartar until frothy. Add the sugar, cinnamon, and nutmeg and beat until stiff peaks form. Drop large spoonfuls of the beaten whites into the simmering milk and poach for a few minutes on each side, turning once, just until they feel firm. Remove carefully with a slotted spoon and drain on paper towels. Let cool slightly. Spread some of the blueberry sauce on a platter or individual plates and top with the islands. Refrigerate until ready to serve and then put a dab of the sauce on each island.

Each serving provides
102 calories   2.8 g protein   15.2 g carbohydrate   3.1 g fat
0.1 g dietary fiber   63 mg sodium   0 mg cholesterol

CHOCOLATE-RASPBERRY CREAM

Makes 8 servings.

You can cut the calories even more if you use nonfat pudding mix, although you will have to cook the nonfat pudding and give it time to cool.

1 (5.9-ounce) package instant chocolate pudding
3 cups nonfat milk
2 tablespoons Chambord liqueur
2 tablespoons seedless raspberry jam

¼ cup nonfat sour cream
⅓ cup whipped dessert topping
Fresh raspberries and fresh mint leaves for garnish (optional)

Put the pudding mix, milk, Chambord, and jam into a blender and blend 1 minute. Remove to a bowl and stir in the sour cream. Spoon into dessert bowls or wine glasses and top each with a dab of the whipped dessert topping, a couple of raspberries, and a mint leaf.

Each serving provides
118 calories   4 g protein   22.8 g carbohydrate   1.1 g fat
0.2 g dietary fiber   252 mg sodium   2 mg cholesterol

QUICK-AND-EASY FRUIT CRISP

Makes 6 servings.

Serve this with a little whipped dessert topping or a scoop of frozen nonfat yogurt.

1 teaspoon almond extract	¼ cup rolled oats
1 (21-ounce) can cherry or blueberry pie filling	2 tablespoons chopped walnuts or pecans
⅓ package white cake mix (save the other ⅔ in your freezer for next time)	2 tablespoons nonfat milk
	1 tablespoon butter

Preheat the oven to 375°F.

Stir the almond extract into the pie filling while it is still in the can. Spread the pie filling in a small baking dish. Put the cake mix, oats, nuts, milk, and butter into a bowl and stir until crumbly. Sprinkle over the pie filling. Bake, uncovered, for 20 to 25 minutes, or until golden.

Each serving provides

280 calories   2.3 g protein   54.2 g carbohydrate   5.9 g fat
10.1 g dietary fiber   191 mg sodium   6 mg cholesterol

BAKED APPLES WITH CALVADOS CREAM

Makes 6 servings.

This is a cozy, old-time dessert. I have delicious memories of it from my childhood.

6 Red Delicious or Golden Delicious apples	½ teaspoon ground cloves
Juice of 2 lemons	¾ cup apple cider
Vegetable oil spray	1 (8-ounce) carton nonfat vanilla or lemon yogurt
¼ cup dried blueberries	3 tablespoons nonfat sour cream
1 cup light brown sugar	
1½ teaspoons cinnamon	2 tablespoons Calvados

Preheat the oven to 375°F.

Core the apples and cut each apple into sixths. As you cut the apples, put them in water with the juice from 1 lemon so they do not turn brown.

Put the apples in an ovenproof dish, such as a 12-inch oval dish, that has been sprayed with vegetable oil. Sprinkle the blueberries over the apples. Put the remaining lemon juice, sugar, cinnamon, cloves, and cider in a saucepan and cook, stirring, until the sugar has dissolved. Pour the sauce over the apples and bake until the apples are soft, about 20 to 25 minutes. Baste the apples about every 10 minutes with the sauce. When done, remove from the oven, and let cool for about 10 minutes.

While the apples cook, mix the yogurt, sour cream, and Calvados together. Spoon some apples on each plate and put a dab of the Calvados mixture on the apples. Drizzle with the brown sugar sauce from the baking dish and enjoy.

Note: If you want a thicker cream for this dish, drain the yogurt in the refrigerator overnight. To do this, put a coffee filter in a mesh strainer and fill it with the yogurt. Place the strainer over a bowl and let this sit in the refrigerator overnight or all day. Pour out the liquid that accumulates in the bowl and use the drained yogurt as directed above.

Each serving provides

323 calories   2.8 g protein   78.4 g carbohydrate   0.7 g fat
4.2 g dietary fiber   55 mg sodium   1 mg cholesterol

FRESH PEACH TART

Makes 8 servings.

Gorgeous fresh peaches baked on store-bought phyllo dough make a scrumptious and easy lowfat dessert. To make the phyllo dough easier to handle, thaw in the refrigerator overnight. The slow defrosting keeps the sheets from tearing as easily.

5 sheets phyllo dough
   Butter-flavored vegetable
   oil spray
1 teaspoon butter
5 large fresh peaches, peeled,
   pitted, and sliced
3 tablespoons brown sugar

Juice of ½ lemon
1 teaspoon fresh lemon zest
1 tablespoon brandy
1 tablespoon granulated
   sugar
1 tablespoon powdered sugar
   for dusting

Preheat oven to 375°F.

Line a rimmed cookie sheet with parchment paper. Take a sheet of the phyllo and lay it flat on the cookie sheet. Spray the phyllo with the butter-flavored vegetable oil. Repeat until you have used all 5 sheets, spraying each time. Fold over 1 inch of the dough to the inside. Fold over once more to make a nice rim for the peaches.

Melt the butter in a skillet. Add the peaches, brown sugar, lemon juice, and zest and cook the peaches carefully, turning once until they soften slightly. Sprinkle on the brandy and let cook 30 seconds more.

Carefully lay the peach slices on the phyllo dough and spoon a little of the sauce on the peaches. Spray the phyllo dough edges with the vegetable oil and sprinkle with the granulated sugar. Bake until the pastry is golden brown, about 18 to 20 minutes. Dust with powdered sugar and serve.

Each serving provides
92 calories   1.3 g protein   18.3 g carbohydrate   1.4 g fat
1.1 g dietary fiber   65 mg sodium   1 mg cholesterol

APPLE-JALAPEÑO CRISP

Makes 12 servings.

You may be skeptical of this combination, but it is fantastic.

2 pounds Rome Beauty or McIntosh apples, peeled and chopped
1 to 2 small, fresh jalapeños, seeds and membranes removed, minced
¼ cup sugar
Juice of 1 lemon

½ cup flour
½ cup sugar
⅓ cup corn flake crumbs
1 teaspoon cinnamon
2 teaspoons butter
2 tablespoons evaporated skim milk

Preheat oven to 400°F.

Toss the apples, jalapeños, sugar, and lemon together and put into a 10-inch pie pan. In a bowl, mix together the flour, sugar, corn flake crumbs, and cinnamon. Cut in the butter and milk. Sprinkle over the apples. Reduce oven heat to 375°F and bake 25 to 30 minutes, or until the top is golden brown.

Each serving provides
115 calories   1 g protein   27.2 g carbohydrate   1 g fat
1.4 g dietary fiber   31 mg sodium   2 mg cholesterol

Index

International Conversion Chart

These are not exact equivalents: they've been slightly rounded to make measuring easier.

LIQUID MEASUREMENTS

American	Imperial	Metric	Australian
2 tablespoons (1 oz.)	1 fl. oz.	30 ml	1 tablespoon
1/4 cup (2 oz.)	2 fl. oz.	60 ml	2 tablespoons
1/3 cup (3 oz.)	3 fl. oz.	80 ml	1/4 cup
1/2 cup (4 oz.)	4 fl. oz.	125 ml	1/3 cup
2/3 cup (5 oz.)	5 fl. oz.	165 ml	1/2 cup
3/4 cup (6 oz.)	6 fl. oz.	185 ml	2/3 cup
1 cup (8 oz.)	8 fl. oz.	250 ml	3/4 cup

SPOON MEASUREMENTS

American	Metric
1/4 teaspoon	1 ml
1/2 teaspoon	2 ml
1 teaspoon	5 ml
1 tablespoon	15 ml

WEIGHTS

US/UK	Metric
1 oz.	30 grams (g)
2 oz.	60 g
4 oz. (1/4 lb)	125 g
5 oz. (1/3 lb)	155 g
6 oz.	185 g
7 oz.	220 g
8 oz. (1/2 lb)	250 g
10 oz.	315 g
12 oz. (3/4 lb)	375 g
14 oz.	440 g
16 oz. (1 lb)	500 g
2 lbs	1 kg

OVEN TEMPERATURES

Farenheit	Centigrade	Gas
250	120	1/2
300	150	2
325	160	3
350	180	4
375	190	5
400	200	6
450	230	8

Good-for-You cookbooks show how to make favorites like pasta, soup, stew, and all kinds of garlic dishes in more healthful ways—without compromising on flavor. Each cookbook offers more than 125 tempting recipes for dishes everyone will love. Every recipe includes a complete nutritional analysis covering fat content, cholesterol, carbohydrates, calories, protein, fiber, and sodium. *Good-for-You* cookbooks bring out the wholesome side of delicious foods!

Easy to Prepare! Complete Nutritional Breakdown with Every Recipe

GOOD·FOR·YOU
PASTA
COOKBOOK
OVER 125 DELICIOUSLY HEALTHFUL RECIPES
LINDA FERRARI

EASY TO PREPARE! COMPLETE NUTRITIONAL BREAKDOWN WITH EVERY RECIPE

GOOD·FOR·YOU
SOUPS & STEWS
COOKBOOK
OVER 125 DELICIOUSLY HEALTHFUL RECIPES
LINDA FERRARI

good gifts from the home

SALSAS, CHUTNEYS & RELISHES

MAKE BEAUTIFUL GIFTS TO GIVE (OR KEEP)

linda ferrari

Salsas, Chutneys & Relishes

Linda Ferrari

*R*evealing the secrets of classic salsas, chutneys, and relishes, Linda Ferrari presents everyone's favorite recipes and a host of thoroughly modern recipes too. Ferrari also presents ways to personalize and decorate your homemade gifts with the distinct love and warmth of a bygone era. Includes recipes for Apple–Walnut Chutney, Festive Cranberry Relish, and Jicama and Chili Salsa.

Jams, Jellies & Preserves

Linda Ferrari

Linda Ferrari shares the secrets of canning the perfect jams, jellies, and preserves as well as innovative ideas for wrapping and packaging so that anyone you present them to will feel charmed, flattered, and loved! Includes recipes for Frangelico Fig Jam, Pomegranate–Kiwi Jelly, Currant and Quince Jam, and Old-Fashioned Blackberry Preserves.

Lighten Up!

Tija Petrovich

*L*ighten Up! presents 150 recipes for tempting, gourmet-quality meals and extras sure to please the discerning palate. Tija Petrovich offers tips on changing from a high-fat to a lowfat lifestyle, stocking the pantry to prevent temptation, eating out, and preparing healthier versions of old favorites. Tija Petrovich is a personal trainer, nutritionist, and former championship bodybuilder. She lives in Seattle, Washington.

PRIMA PUBLISHING
P.O. Box 1260BK   Rocklin, CA 95677

USE YOUR VISA/MC AND ORDER BY PHONE
(916) 632-4400

Monday–Friday 9 A.M.–4 P.M. PST

I'd like to order copies of the following titles:

Quantity	Title	Amount
_____	Good-for-You Pasta Cookbook $14.95	_____
_____	Good-for-You Soups and Stews Cookbook $12.95	_____
_____	Good-for-You Garlic Cookbook $12.95	_____
_____	Salsas, Chutneys & Relishes $12.00	_____
_____	Jams, Jellies & Preserves $12.00	_____
_____	Lighten Up! $16.95	_____
_____	_____	_____
_____	_____	_____

Subtotal _____

Postage & Handling* _____

Sales Tax: 7.25% (CA); 5% (IN and MD); 8.25% (TN) _____

TOTAL (U.S. funds only) _____

Check enclosed for $ _____(payable to Prima Publishing)

HAWAII, ALASKA, CANADA, FOREIGN, AND PRIORITY REQUEST
ORDERS, PLEASE CALL ORDER ENTRY FOR PRICE QUOTE (916) 632-4400

Charge my   ❏ MasterCard   ❏ Visa

Account No. _____ Exp. Date _____

Print Your Name _____

Your Signature _____

Address _____

City/State/Zip _____

Daytime Telephone (___) _____

*Postage & Handling
Purchase Amount: Add:
$14.99 or less $3.00
$15–$29.99..........$4.00
$30–$49.99..........$6.00
$50–$99.99........$10.00
$100 –$199.99....$13.50

Prices are subject to change.

Please allow three to four weeks for delivery.